AF660091

the 5 Things We Need to be Happy

and money isn't one of them

the 5 Things We Need to be Happy

and money isn't one of them

Patricia Lorenz

JAICO PUBLISHING HOUSE

Ahmedabad Bangalore Bhopal Bhubaneswar Chennai
Delhi Hyderabad Kolkata Lucknow Mumbai

Published by Jaico Publishing House
A-2 Jash Chambers, 7-A Sir Phirozshah Mehta Road
Fort, Mumbai - 400 001
jaicopub@jaicobooks.com
www.jaicobooks.com

Published in arrangement with
Guideposts
110 William Street, 9th floor
New York, NY 10038, USA

THE 5 THINGS WE NEED TO BE HAPPY
ISBN 978-81-8495-268-1

First Jaico Impression: 2011

Printed by
Repro India Limited
Plot No. 50/2, T.T.C. MIDC Industrial Area
Mahape, Navi Mumbai - 400 710.

Thank you . . .

To my entire family scattered about in Illinois, California, Wisconsin, Ohio, Kentucky and Alaska: Dad, Bev, Jeanne, Canyon, Adeline, Julia, Hailey, Riley, Casey, Michael, Amy, Hannah, Zachary, Chloe, Andrew, Carrissa, Ethan, Joe, Linda, Aaron, Kirstie, Mark, Brody, Anna, Catherine, Bill and Sarah. You have all had a hand in showing me the five ingredients to happiness and supported me in my decision not to include money as a major factor in my life.

To my good friends in just as many states from all the stages of my life. You have all inspired me to keep writing and to treasure the five things we need to be happy.

To everyone at Guideposts, thank you for your hard work on this and every book you publish. It's gratifying to be part of the family of books that inspire so many.

To all the people I wrote about in this book. Thank you for sharing.

To Jack, who lives just fifty-seven steps from my home in Florida and who shares my life and my love and encourages me daily to enjoy all five of the things that make us happy.

—Patricia Lorenz

Contents

Introduction

I am not an expert in anything. I don't have a master's degree or a PhD. I have a simple BA degree in English, not even a teaching certificate. I'm not a licensed professional. I don't have a clinical background. I haven't studied abroad.

But I have traveled, read and experienced life to the best of my ability. I've raised four children, mostly as a single parent. Like many other ordinary people, I know a little bit about a lot of things, but not a whole lot about any one thing. I'm your average woman who lives life simply, one week at a time, just like you do.

I'm not gorgeous, nor do I spend hours every day trying to be. I wear very little make-up and keep my hair short because it's easier that way. And, okay, if you want to know the truth, I bite my fingernails but every so often when I forget about them and they grow, I love nothing better than going to one of those inexpensive nail places and getting a manicure for ten or twelve dollars.

I've been trying to lose the same twenty-five pounds my entire adult life. I lose ten, gain five, lose five, gain ten. But I do exercise every day—at least on the weekdays. Usually it's an hour of water aerobics in the pool across the street, or an eight-mile bike ride to my favorite park and back. But the thing is, I don't obsess about exercise or food. I do my best, but I don't waste time beating myself up if I have a hot fudge sundae every now and then.

I have relatives and friends who love me, a small, stress-free condo that's paid for, and the Florida sun, beaches and swimming pools to enchant me twelve months a year.

As a single woman who was head of her household for nineteen years in Wisconsin I find I now like living alone. I've become so accustomed to the quiet and solitude necessary to write that spending large blocks of time alone is one of my greatest joys. I think you have to be intrinsically happy to be able to enjoy solitude.

With all my heart, I'm proclaiming here and now that I'm one of the happiest people I know. These past sixty-plus years have given me some of the answers to the happiness questions. I've figured out what it takes to be happy. I hope that if I share what I've discovered, it will help you feel happier as well.

Believe me, it isn't money that makes us happy. I don't have a lot of money; never have. I've made less than twenty thousand dollars a year for all but four years of my life, and even then I earned under twenty-eight thousand. But so far I've lived an interesting, fulfilling, happy, stress-free life with more adventures than most of my friends who have lots more money than I.

It helps that I'm a frugal soul who still looks for restaurant coupons in the paper, buys many of her clothes at consignment shops and enjoys the thrill of a good bargain. I'll buy two boxes of the same kind of cereal if the sign says Buy One, Get One Free. But the main ingredients of happiness have nothing to do with being frugal—or with money at all, for that matter.

I hope I'm at—or perhaps just past—the halfway point in my life and can enjoy real happiness for many more years. I'd love to live to be 110 . . . as long as I can still feed myself, get around with a walker, see and hear well enough to communicate and be of some value to those around me.

But who knows? My dad is still happy, active and thriving at age eighty-eight. So far I've had sixty-two mostly happy years. The few years that weren't so happy were at least interesting and productive. And those were the years that taught me how to love my struggles. I believe that having mostly happy years is enough experience to write a book.

My experiences have taught me that nothing makes us happy that is outside of ourselves. Nothing. Not money, good health, free time, other people, luxuries, being in control or being successful in business or finance. Happiness comes from within. It's a state of mind, an attitude.

How do I know this? Because I've met people who are very happy yet poor as a gerbil spinning a wheel in a tiny cage. Being successful can only make you happy as long as the happiness comes from doing something with the talents you were given at birth. If it's money that drives you, chances are you are not truly, intrinsically happy.

So many times when people become wealthy, their lives become so stressful and busy that they barely have time to tie their shoes, let alone step back and actually enjoy their success. The pressure is so great that they can't "leave" work for one minute, even when they're on the golf course or at home with their families. Their cell phones, computers, Powerbooks, Palm Pilots and other electronic gadgetry make sure that they're never more than a click away from *running things.*

Another lesson I've learned about happiness is that it doesn't matter what's ahead for us in this great scheme of things. What matters is whether or not we're happy today—right now. Are you? I am. I really, truly am.

I was raised in a happy two-parent family in the Midwest, had hardworking parents who taught me good values. I graduated from college, have been married, divorced and annulled twice, lived in five different states and raised four children on a shoestring.

Because of a sister-in-law who worked for the airlines and the crash pad for forty airline pilots I ran after three of my children were out on their own, I was able to travel on airline "friend passes" for pennies on the dollar for many years. I've seen much of the world and have had amazing adventures. However, it wasn't the adventures that made me happy; it was having the freedom and the determination to never say no to an opportunity.

Our ability to be happy is often clouded by worry, stress, despair, fear or not being able to forgive or ask for forgiveness. When those things hung over my head like a huge black umbrella, I fixed it. I talked to friends, got counseling, prayed, wrote about my feelings, sorted things out logistically, then often I took a vacation, even if it was only an afternoon at the library, to make sure I wasn't running on empty. I just knew I had to get rid of those negative things in my life because life is very short.

The only person who can make me happy is me. It's not fair to blame someone else or lots of someones if I think I'm unhappy. Because it's not their job. The job of making me happy is mine alone. The job of making you happy is up to you.

There are, however, five ingredients that make your quest for happiness not only easier, but practically a certainty. I hope, as you read this book, that you will be surprised by these five things and delight in their simplicity.

Over the years I've asked many people what they think the five ingredients of happiness are, and, invariably, they blurt out, "Lots of money"; "a bigger retirement fund." Or they name things money can buy: "A bigger house"; "a Rolls Royce"; "a trip around the world"; "a yacht"; "real diamonds"; "a maid." Or they go on about the Miss America dreams: "Peace in the world"; "no more war"; "better health"; "cures for diseases."

Once at a company Christmas party, a woman's hand shot up when I asked the question during an after-dinner speech I was giving. She giggled, then shouted, "Great sex! That's important if you're really going to be happy."

An older woman at a church group said good health had to be one of the most important ingredients of real happiness. I had to remind her that we all know people who don't have good health or are physically challenged in some way and yet are quite happy with their lives.

I truly believe that the five things you'll learn about in this book are the core ingredients of a happy life. You may be asking, "What happens when life throws me a curve? What happens when a loved one gets cancer? Or teenagers are brutally slaughtered by one of their own? Or a loved one gets involved in drugs? Or a marriage fails? How do you find happiness as a refugee in a country where tens of thousands of people are pushed out of their homes by enemy soldiers? How can people be happy who lose their homes because of the raging fury of devastating tornadoes, hurricanes, floods or earthquakes?"

How do you find happiness when life throws a curve? The same way you find happiness on a normal day when the sun is shining and the boss is happy and your spouse not only did the laundry last night but gave you a huge hug before you left that morning. You simply grab onto the five ingredients for happiness with even more grit and determination. When you're caught in the midst of a gullywashing nightmare in life, that is when you really need someone to love more than any other time. When the chips are down is when you need something to do to begin to repair and rebuild. When life seems at its bleakest is when we must have something to hope for on a grand scale. Something to believe in makes it possible to go on.

And something to laugh at makes the journey worthwhile and fun.

I believe with all my heart that if we have these five ingredients our lives will naturally be happy. The best thing is that all five are easily attainable. All five start from deep within ourselves and grow and flourish until our happiness quotient bubbles up and out and becomes contagious. Before you know it, not only are you happy, but you're helping to make others happy as well. What a concept!

Chapter One

Why Money Isn't One of Them

There's nothing in the world so demoralizing as money.
—*Sophocles*

Adults often ask children, "What do you want to be when you grow up? What do you want to accomplish? What are your dreams, goals, hopes for the future? What's going to make you happy?"

We expect kids to know the answers. They think they know the answers but they don't. What about you? What will make you happy? When asked that question most adults say, "More money. That'll make me happy." Trouble is, when you start looking at rich people's lives, most of them are so busy making money and more money, and then more and more money, that they really don't have time to be happy and enjoy life.

A study was done many years ago in which people who earned twenty thousand dollars a year were asked, "Is that enough money?" The answer was a resounding "No."

So then they interviewed a group of people who earned forty thousand a year. "Is that enough money?" Again, the answer was, "No."

In the next group in the study each person earned eighty thousand a year. They were asked, "Is that enough money?" Every person in the study said, "No, it's not."

See the pattern here? They asked people who earned one hundred fifty thousand a year if that was enough. It wasn't. Even those who made a quarter or half a million dollars said it wasn't sufficient.

It's never enough money. Make no mistake. When it comes to the ingredients of happiness, money is not one of them. And since no amount of money seems to be enough for people, it stands to reason that money is not the cause or the root of happiness. The people who earned eighty thousand a year weren't any happier than those who earned twenty thousand. Those with half a million dollars were no more content than those who earned forty thousand a year.

I was taking a class in the mid eighties when I heard about this money study. After the professor told us about it he asked, "How much money is enough to make people happy, do you think?" I was sitting in the back of the room, a single parent raising four children with a thirty-hour-a-week job. I gingerly raised my hand. "I make ten thousand dollars a year, and I think that's enough. I'm happy. I have lots of reasons to be happy. I'm healthy. I have four healthy children. I have an interesting job. I have good friends. Faith in God. A nice home. Lots of laughs. I have many blessings and I'm very happy." It was the first time in my life that I realized I was happy . . . really, truly happy.

Treasures of the Heart

A few years after that experience with the professor, I began to look around my house, noticing how many things I'd collected over the years: antique furniture, unusual napkin rings, hundred-year-old hat pins, beach glass, old crocks, glassware, brass and silver. But I started to notice a heavy feeling whenever I looked at my collections. I wasn't sure why, but the fun had gone out of collecting.

Why do I have so many things? I'd ask myself.

Then, surprisingly, I'd answer right back: *They're your treasures. Keepsakes. Things to pass on to your children and grandchildren. Besides, they're fun to look at and display.*

But something happened in 1993 that made me see my collections in a whole different light. I was in Louisville, Kentucky, visiting my only brother Joe and my sister-in-law Linda. One day we three attended an auction sale . . . a little slice of heaven for a collector like me. The newspaper ad proclaimed it to be "The Lifetime Collection of Donald and Janet Dixon."

I wondered if Mr. and Mrs. Dixon were paring down their possessions before moving into a retirement home. I wondered if perhaps one of them had died recently.

What Joe, Linda and I discovered when we pulled into the driveway was that Donald and Janet Dixon were millionaires. Their house, on acres and acres of perfectly manicured grounds, complete with a pool and Jacuzzi, had sold to the first looker for $650,000. This was in 1993, remember. All of their exquisite possessions were sitting on the front lawn under huge tents, waiting to be sold at public auction. More than four hundred items worth hundreds of thousands of dollars were cataloged on the legal-size sheets given to each of the many potential bidders on that hot June afternoon.

The list included a "highly carved Chippendale mahogany

kingsize four-post canopy bed on claw feet," a "superb Queen Anne burl walnut bookcase-china cabinet with beveled glass doors, dated 1890," a "mother-of-pearl inlaid rosewood tea caddy with hinged box interior, circa 1850," a "rare signed Tiffany and Company coffee urn" and a "three-piece Ansonia marble clock set with open encasement and mercury pendulum, circa 1880."

This wasn't your typical auction sale. The Dixons' auction also included a Mercedes Benz automobile in superb condition; a six-month-old snazzy red pick-up truck; and an Audi 200 Quattro Turbo with heated seats. The Dixons were selling everything, including the wheels right out from under themselves.

"Why would anyone part with all their treasures?" I asked Linda. She shrugged her shoulders, obviously as mystified as I was, and said, "Look at the china, candelabra and cut glass. Think of the parties these people had!"

I ran my fingers over the fine sharp edges of half-a-dozen huge cut-glass vases and umbrella stands. As I walked around a dozen antique Persian rugs stretched out on the lawn, I tried to imagine why or how one could give up such beauty.

The auction began under another giant tent filled with folding chairs out on the south lawn. The Dixons pristine navy-blue leather sofa sold to the highest bidder for just under two thousand dollars. The huge mahogany dining room table sold for fifteen hundred. The twelve matching chairs went for $265 each. This definitely wasn't a sale for faint-of-pocketbook folks like me.

Why, I wondered over and over, *Why would they sell it all? Don't they have children who would want these treasures?* Certainly many of the antiques had been in their families for generations.

We left after three hours before a third of the items had been sold. My brother managed to get a dandy oak workbench for fifty dollars, something the antique dealers weren't interested in. The next morning when we went back to the Dixons to pick up the workbench, my curiosity got the better of me. I just *had* to know why Donald and Janet Dixon were selling their home and all those exquisite furnishings, antiques and treasures.

When I rang the doorbell a pretty young woman with long, light brown, wavy hair, no makeup and simple clothes answered. *Wow, they even have a maid,* I thought to myself wistfully.

"Is Mrs. Dixon home?" I asked.

"I'm Mrs. Dixon," she said simply, flashing a warm smile.

"Oh my goodness," I stammered. "Forgive me, I don't mean to intrude, but, well, I'm here with my brother. He's out in the garage loading the workbench he bought yesterday. I just had to meet you. I'm wondering if you would mind telling me why you sold all your beautiful possessions."

Mrs. Dixon graciously invited me into their home and introduced me to her husband who reminded Janet that they had to be at the house closing in forty-five minutes.

I repeated my question to Mr. Dixon, "How could you sell all your beautiful treasures?"

Mr. Dixon, a good-looking, curly-haired man in his early forties, smiled, put his arm around his wife's waist and said quietly. "Oh, I *didn't* sell my treasures. All that is just *stuff*. My treasures are right here; my wife and daughter. Have you met our daughter, Collyn? She's eleven. Yes, these are my treasures, Janet and Collyn. They're all I need."

Mrs. Dixon explained that the previous April she had gone to the Bahamas for a week with a friend and fell in love with a tiny island called Green Turtle Cay in Abaco. She called her husband and asked him to join her so he could see the beauty of the tiny island. Donald flew over the next day and together they explored the island, befriended the natives and thoroughly relaxed in a world that had missed out on the twentieth century. After a few days Janet and Donald decided to change their lives. They agreed to sell their home and all their possessions and move to the Bahamas with nothing but their bathing suits and a few small personal items.

Janet's eyes danced with excitement. "We're leaving tonight, can you believe it? Tomorrow our address will be Green Turtle Cay. We're moving into an old, simple, one-story oceanside home with just four rooms: a kitchen, a living room and two bedrooms. No phone or TV. In fact, there are only two pay phones on the whole island. It takes three weeks for mail to get from here to there.

"We're really looking forward to just spending time together. This life here, these things, the big house, all those furnishings and stuff, the Junior League, it's just not me. I don't like what happens to your life when you have money. Things somehow become more important than people. This house and all those expensive items are not important. What's really important is family, sunshine, wind and the sea, and those will be the things we'll have every day on the island."

When I came home from Louisville, I started cleaning house. I gathered up hundreds of items for a rummage sale. I wrapped up a cherished silver casserole dish and two collectible green vases that my sister-in-law had admired and shipped them off to her.

I gift-wrapped a set of antique butter plates that had been in my family for three generations and gave them to a neighbor couple who had just gotten married. I gave my brass collection to my son for Christmas. I placed one hundred and fifty books on my dining room table and insisted that friends in my women's group each take a handful home with them. I gave most of my silver collection to my four children. The next spring I put over a hundred items on a big table out by the street in front of my house with a huge sign that simply said Free.

When I moved from Wisconsin to Florida, I sold and gave away two-thirds of all my possessions. Granted, moving from a large six-bedroom home to a two-bedroom condo one third its size forced me to get rid of things, but when it was all over I felt a huge sense of freedom, a cleansing of sorts. It was fun to see how much the people who received my things enjoyed them, but the best part was that when I stopped collecting and started giving away instead, I had less clutter around me to dust, which meant I had more time to spend with my friends and family. And those, as the Dixons taught me, are my real treasures.

Twice the Life on Half the Money

Another couple I met while living in Milwaukee taught me a valuable lesson about money. Art and Karen Beaudry shared this story with me at a point in my life where I was coming to grips with the fact that I was in a profession that wasn't financially secure. I loved working at home, writing and preparing speeches: The work itself made me happy, and the freedom was delicious. I had plenty of time to spend with my children. But the money stunk. Then I met Art and Karen. Their story changed my life.

The early morning sun bounced blue, honey-brown and red light through the stained glass windows in Art and Karen's dining room one spring Monday in 1989, but the two of them were too grouchy to enjoy it. They sat at the table with their usual "wake me up" breakfast, strong black coffee and bagels.

Art looked at Karen and saw lines of stress on her face and dark, swollen bags under her eyes. She had another cold, and her crabbiness pushed through the air like a steel wedge.

"I can't believe it's Monday already," she grumbled. "I hate getting up this early."

Art fiddled with his bagel, trying to avoid his wife's eyes. Lately, all their weekday mornings were like that. As full-time librarians for the Milwaukee public library system their work days were crammed with books, bosses, do this, do that, ringing phones, forms, budgets, trying to help the general public eight hours a day and never-enough-time-to-get-it-all-done stress. Their weekends were crammed with cooking, cleaning, shopping, housework, yard work, home repairs, errands, visiting Art's parents, rushing here, rushing there.

Art's mother would call and ask him to come over for a visit or to help with some little thing. He was ashamed to admit how many times he begged off. Or he'd get a call from a school to come and tell stories to the children, something he truly loved to do, but he'd turn them down because he had too much work to do at the library.

Art also tinkered with the idea of getting into politics, but, naturally, that ambition was squashed. Not enough time. Slowly, insidiously, over the past fifteen years, the joy had gone out of their lives.

Art closed his eyes for a minute, trying to remember days when they were really happy. He couldn't remember many, but he forced a smile and reached out to touch his wife's hand. She pulled her hand away.

"Karen, I know you're miserable. I'm not happy either. We simply have no time to do anything we really want to do with our lives."

Karen nodded. "Art, we're each making forty thousand dollars a year but we don't even have time to *spend* that money, let alone enjoy it."

Karen had tried to transfer out of her department four times, but no transfers were available. In addition to never having enough time to enjoy life, Karen's frequent headaches, stomach problems and asthma attacks had become a way of life for her.

Art glanced at the stained glass rainbow dancing on the wall, then at his wife who had just grumbled about something else and finally said out loud what he'd been thinking for weeks.

"Karen, no job in the world is worth all this. Why don't you just quit? I've been thinking and praying about this a lot lately. I think I found the answer in Deuteronomy 8:3." Art opened his Bible and read the verse to his wife:

> *Yes, he humbled you by letting you go hungry and then feeding you with manna, a food previously unknown to both you and your ancestors. He did it to help you realize that food isn't everything, and that real life comes by obeying every command of God. (TLB)*

"Our problem," Art said slowly, "is that we have too much bread and no real life. We aren't developing the talents God gave us. We're too busy making money."

Art took a deep breath and continued. "Why can't we share my job as equal partners? Then we'd each have time to develop those things that are really important."

Karen raised her head and looked right into her husband's eyes. "Quit my job? Work part-time doing *your* job? What a crazy idea!"

She turned her head and stared out the window. Finally she spoke again. "*Hmm.* You know I do have children's library experience. How would it work, sharing a job with you? Do you really think we could get by on half as much money?"

"Karen, I believe God will take care of us financially, and in every way possible, if we just do this in faith and start using the talents God has given us."

"I'm not so sure I have any talents," Karen said skeptically.

For the next few days Art and Karen talked about how they could make a job-share work. They knew they'd have to have most of the details hammered out before presenting the idea to Art's boss.

On the big day, Art's boss had quite a few questions, but Art and his wife were prepared. Over the next few weeks Art's boss agreed to the entire plan, including the part where Art would work one week and Karen would work the next. They agreed to share one set of benefits. They told the boss that if something came up and one of them needed to be away from the library for a few days during their regular work week, the other would fill in. Art's boss said it wouldn't matter which one of them came to work on any given day or week, as long as they both put in the same number of hours each year.

Not long after they began sharing one job, Art took three months off to run for alderman. Karen stepped in and worked those three months full-time. Art lost the election, then worked three months straight so Karen could stay home and work at some creative projects she'd been longing to try.

After that, on his off weeks, Art started visiting schools and libraries out of state to do something he'd always dreamed about—tell stories to children. He got requests from schools all over the Midwest and even as far away as Las Vegas.

Best of all, on the days when he was working, he'd come home and find Karen bent over the dining room table carefully practicing her calligraphy for the class she was taking.

"Hi, Art! How was work?" Karen would say cheerfully when Art walked in the door. Or Art might find her working on a sculpture or painting, drawing or weaving a basket.

Art's wife was a new woman whose talents were blossoming as she took one art class after another.

When Art was off work he developed his hobby of origami, the ancient art of Japanese paper folding. He spent long luxurious hours creating intricate folded paper masterpieces, then began teaching origami to various groups.

As the whole mood in their house changed, Art and Karen both found more time to spend together, doing special things for each other. Often when she was working at the library he'd surprise her with a special dinner, including fresh flowers on the table.

"Welcome to the Beaudry Café," he'd say with a flourish when she'd walk in the door after work. "There's homemade pasta and one of my special back rubs for dessert!"

Art says that the smile on his wife's face and their good-natured conversations every day made up for the change in their income a hundredfold.

Another longtime dream of Art's was to be a hospital chaplain. After taking classes and then volunteering his services here and there for three years, he was given a regular eight-hour-a-week position as a chaplain at one of Milwaukee's largest hospitals.

A few years later Art and Karen even took their dream-of-a-lifetime trip to Europe. The leap of faith they made in combining their two jobs into one had paid off in so many ways that they could hardly believe how wonderfully their lives changed. It seemed that the good Lord had given them more blessings than they'd ever dreamed.

As a result of their job-sharing, Art had enough time to help his parents reorganize their financial and medical records. His mother often traveled with him when he went on storytelling trips, and the two of them developed a friendship Art said he wouldn't trade for anything.

A few years after their job-sharing began, Karen mentioned how much she was enjoying teaching her ninth- and tenth-grade religious education classes. Art had never heard her say that before they cut their jobs in half. She also spent more time exploring her own relationship with God. She read spiritual classics as well as the Bible and, more importantly, she had time to think about them. How many people in today's world have time to sit and think?

In 1994, when Art and Karen celebrated their twentieth anniversary at the library, the deputy librarian for the entire Milwaukee public library system came to the branch library where they worked to give them their twenty-year pins. All the employees gathered in the staff room for cake and conversation. Their boss stood up and said, "We have an unusual system here, a married couple sharing one job. It's so good for the library. They each bring different talents and strengths to the position, and since they started their job-sharing in 1989, they haven't missed one day of work."

Not long after that Art told the students in his confirmation classes, "We have to celebrate the gifts and talents God has given us. We must use them! That means I *must* live my faith by being a storyteller, paper-folder, hospital chaplain and religious education teacher. It means my wife *must* live her faith by taking art classes, studying the Bible and exploring her own personal growth. She's very talented at needlepoint and gardening. Because she has time to do these things, she's a very happy woman."

So many times in his work at the hospital or teaching Sunday school, Art hears the same thing: "Oh, I'm not talented at anything. I always wanted to learn to play the piano, paint, dance, whatever, but I don't have any talent." He tells those people, "Of course you have talent! God gave everyone talent. You just need time to find out what it is and time to do it, that's all."

One morning during one of their long luxurious breakfasts when Art didn't have to go to work until noon, he and Karen laughed at the stained-glass rainbow dancing on the wall. Then Karen reached for Art's hand.

"You know, Art, right now, while I'm still young I'm living dreams I thought I wouldn't get to until I was much older and retired."

She squeezed his hand, smiled and continued. "The other day I was returning to my desk at work after helping a child with some information for a school project. Tiffany, a little fourth grade girl with black braids and big brown eyes, stopped me and asked, 'Why are you always smiling?'

"At first, Tiffany's question caught me off guard because I hadn't realized I smiled so much. I thought for a second and then simply told the truth.

"It's because I'm so happy, Tiffany."

Karen and Art both agree wholeheartedly that the human spirit does not live by bread alone, and when it comes right down to it, you certainly *can* have twice the life on half the money.

So You Want to Be Rich?

Over the years I've watched many of my relatives and friends get richer and richer, including one cousin who made hundreds of millions of dollars both here and abroad. During that time a friend invited me to attend one of those self-esteem seminars where they teach you how to be successful.

A thirty-four-year-old man with no college education stepped up to the podium. "By the time I was twenty-two years old I'd had thirty-three different jobs, all minimum wage. One day after hearing a motivational tape I changed my attitude about life, worked my way up in a software company, and a dozen years later, I'm the president of this corporation with an annual salary in the millions. *Two commas!* A two-comma income! Imagine that!"

He raved about his big house, huge yard, boat, fancy cars and his two-comma income. He tried to convince his audience that we too could be just like him. If we sold his product, we too could earn two-comma incomes.

For most of the people in that audience, earning a two-comma income was about as likely as setting foot on Mars. Or my becoming a pro-golfer, considering that I've never played in my life and have no desire to learn.

The same week I heard that speech, three friends and I sat in the small kitchen of one woman in the group, eating a simple late evening supper of ham sandwiches and watermelon. We'd just been to a free summer concert in the park. An Irish family, two brothers and their five children, played Irish folk tunes for two hours. It was wonderful. *What a way for kids to grow up,* I thought as I watched those smiling teenagers and their fathers make the audience laugh, sing, tap their toes, clap their hands. Kids played in the grass near the gazebo. It was what America and good values are all about—families spending time together. Our simple little supper afterward was about good friends spending time together.

As we sat there in that kitchen I asked a question of my three friends: "If you suddenly had the power to be rich, what would happen to your life?" We quickly came up with a list of a dozen not-too-positive things that would make our lives different.

1 Security Inconvenience.

You'd move to a huge house in a fancy neighborhood, a neighborhood where they tell you whether you can put up a fence and what colors you can choose from to paint your own house. Instead of leaving the backdoor unlocked so the kids could come in and out, you'd have a security system as elaborate as Fort Knox. Every time you left the property you'd have to remember your security codes. And sometimes you'd accidentally set off the alarm and frighten the whole neighborhood with the shrieking siren.

2 Communication Stress.

One of the first things the rich learn after pulling down a six-figure salary or a two-comma income is that they can never answer their phone without checking the answering machine or the caller ID. Why? Too many phone solicitations. Every week, dozens of calls from people wanting to sell them investments, home improvements, exotic vacations or banking services. Or credit card companies trying to get them to sign up for their card. Or insurance pitches.

3 The Suits.

Suddenly you've got bankers, accountants, lawyers, insurance agents, tax preparers and realtors all taking up your time. The subject of your money, where it goes, how to spend it, how much to save, how much to spend, what to buy now, and what to invest in later become a huge part of your life. Stocks, bonds, mutual funds, IRAs, investments, divestitures, taxes, deferments and retirement plans become part of your daily vocabulary. The more you have, the more you make and it's a nightmare of organization to keep it all straight.

4 Donations.

Churches, organizations, schools, colleges, clubs, councils, performing arts, ad infinitum know that you're on the list of the rich-and-getting-richer, and you're one of the first people they hit up for donations. They want yearly, monthly, weekly donations. Just the time it takes to open their solicitation envelopes and listen to their spiels on the phone takes away valuable living-happy time. You suddenly start going to opera and ballet fundraisers because that's what rich people do for fun. And that's where the rich go to hobnob with their new friends, other rich people. Instead of Oprah, you now have to watch opera. Don't get me wrong. There's certainly nothing bad about opera or ballet, if you really, truly enjoy it. But if you'd prefer a game of water-balloon tag in the backyard on a hot summer day, well, forget it. No more parties with your favorite band of rowdy friends. No more six-hour picnics in your favorite state park. You're too busy attending formal fundraisers for big charities and picking up your tux and evening gown at the cleaners.

5 Picking Up the Tab.

When you're rich you're expected to pick up the tab, especially when you're with people who aren't as rich as you are. Most non-rich people don't even argue when the check comes and the rich guy reaches for it. The non-rich folks figure time after time that since they've only got a one-comma income, the rich guy can afford it.

6 No Privacy.

The cleaning lady is there once a week. The gardener, the tree trimmer, the landscaper, the architect planning your next building project, the decorator, the woman who makes draperies, the party planner, the plumber fixing the swimming pool and the hot tub and the family attorney who drops in on his way home from work to drop off those papers are all running in and out of your home at all hours of the day and night. Run through the house in your underwear? Take an afternoon nap? Or enjoy a bowl of popcorn in the early evening with the kids while you watch a movie? Kiss it good-bye. There are too many people running around the place fixing, cleaning, preparing, measuring, remodeling and planning to give you any real privacy ever again.

7 No Rest.

One of the truest truisms of all is this: The rich get richer. Period. Once you have money, something happens and you forget everything else but how to make more money. A ton isn't enough. A boxcar full or a shipload isn't enough. You keep moving up the ladder. Now you're having dinner with Michael Jordan's mother. Next, it's an invitation to the White House. Bigger, better, more. Did you ever hear a millionaire say, "I've got enough and from now on I'm going to give every dollar I make to those who don't have as much as I do." Do you know any millionaires who own big rope hammocks and actually use them on a regular basis? Of course not. They're too busy making more money.

8 No Time.

Think about all the things you do now with your kids, significant other, relatives, friends, neighbors. You spend most of the year planning, saving for and dreaming about your two-week vacation. You make every day of that skimpy two-week vacation count. You take lots of pictures and remember the fun for years. In between you wish you had more time to hang out with your friends, grill brats, play cards, fly kites, ride bikes, bake cakes, swim in lakes, go bowling and watch football. You work hard, but you don't play enough. Worrying about how to invest that one hundred thousand stock-option deal just isn't part of your weekend plans.

Meetings, schmeetings, who needs 'em? Don't we all have more important things to do like blowing bubbles with our kids or grandkids, packing the car for that free Saturday night concert or magic show in the park and catching fireflies after the fireworks on the Fourth of July?

9 Friends Change.

When you get rich your friends change. Everybody who's anybody wants to be your friend so instead of getting invited to the neighbor's to cook hot dogs on the grill, you're invited to a black-tie dinner at the Goldwaters', complete with a guest appearance by Japan's most talented seven-year-old Suzuki violin player. Then, of course, you must invite the Goldwaters and all the new friends you just made at their party to a party in your home.

No longer is it acceptable to let Ronald McDonald host your kids' birthday parties. No, when you're rich you have to rent a horse and an inflatable jumping house, hire

Blimpy the Clown, a real cowboy and a country-western singer, and invite all the children of your personal banker, attorney, accountant, boss and board of directors. Cousin Ralph, who always wears his pants too high, and Luella, the fun-loving neighbor from your old neighborhood who still wears flowered polyester pantsuits, just wouldn't fit in anymore. What on earth, you say to yourself, would they ever find to talk about with the Episcopal bishop, the mayor, and Ann-Margret?

10 No More Simple Values and Work Ethic.

When you're rich it's difficult to teach your children simple values and a work ethic because so many of the people in your life don't have any. And if you try you come off looking like Scrooge himself. How can you make your daughter work for her college education if great-grandmother left her a college trust fund worth two hundred thousand dollars? How do you teach children to be self-sufficient when their every need is met from infancy on up? How do you teach children the value of hard work, when they can spend all their time at the beach in the red sports cars that Grandma Old Money gave them for their sixteenth birthday, or watching four or five movies a day with their friends in the family entertainment center on the bigscreen TV or shopping at the fanciest malls with open charge accounts from their parents? And how do they learn to share when, if there are two or more children in the family, the parents buy doubles or triples of everything to avoid squabbles?

11 The Marriage Trap.

If only one of you comes from a rich family, your marriage may be in constant jeopardy. Can't you just hear the first big fight between a couple where the wife is from wealth and the husband isn't? "You better treat me like a queen or you're out of here. I've got Daddy's money and I don't need you to support me or the children." Or, if the situation is reversed, "You'll do as I say, dress the way I tell you, be where I want you to be at every function or you can leave. Just remember the premarital agreement, honey. You're only rich as long as you're married to me." It's nothing more than the life of a kept slave!

12 Loss of Creativity.

If you can simply buy everything you need or want, the joy that comes from being creative is diminished. You lose the special thrill of coordinating your wardrobe with inexpensive items from thrift stores. Enjoy making arts and crafts so you can boost your income? Many rich people rarely have the time to make things. They buy them. Search for inexpensive, creative ways to take the whole family on vacation? Forget it. Go camping to save money? Get real. Bike to work to save a few bucks? The idea will never cross your mind if you have a two-comma income.

If you do inherit or earn a two-comma income, you may want to think about living way beneath your means. Simple is better. Less is more. The only real millionaires are those who give away their money so they can maintain the life most of us already have: a life filled with time for our spouses, children, parents, brothers, sisters, neighbors and friends. Time for those we care about is the only commodity in life that's worth anything. What we all need is time to throw the aluminum lawn chair in the back of the ten-year-old station wagon and head for the free band concert in the park. Don't forget the lemonade.

My Best Sale Ever

One thing rich people rarely do is take part in one of America's greatest pastimes, the rummage-garage-tag-yard-estate sale. They're everywhere, with bargains galore, and the fun of scoring a great deal can only be enjoyed if you really need to save the money. Talk about a shopper's paradise!

Drive through any small town or big-city neighborhood, and you'll wonder if we Americans aren't the rummage-sale capitalists of the world. On Fridays and Saturdays it seems that there's a sale of some sort on every block in every town.

I've hosted at least fifteen garage sales over the years. It's work—hard work. Clean out the garage. Set up tables, most of them makeshift things made out of saw horses and old doors. Unpack the boxes of stuff, price everything, make signs, post them, put an ad in the local paper, then on sale day lug half of your wares out onto the driveway close to the street so nobody going past will miss the fact that you're having a rummage sale.

Then comes the real work: sitting there all day, collecting money, worrying if somebody will steal the money box when you're not looking. Of course, your day starts in the wee hours when the doorbell rings at 6:30 AM and it's somebody who read your ad in the paper.

"Isn't your sale open yet?"

"No, not yet. It opens at eight," you sputter as you pry open your eyes.

"Oh no! I'm on my way to work. Couldn't I please have a peek inside the garage? I won't take long."

After you push the garage-door button, you scramble to the bedroom, throw on some work clothes, pour water in the teapot and rush outside just in time to see the stranger walking toward her car empty-handed.

And so it goes. Some hours you have twenty people shoving each other around in between the too-tight aisles amid your trash and treasures. By midday you're so hot, tired and cranky from arguing prices with every customer who thinks haggling is a national pastime that you're ready to close up shop in favor of a hot bath.

That's how my past rummage sales went. But not anymore. I developed a new method of having rummage sales, one that allowed me to set up in twenty minutes or less; one that requires no advertising; one that doesn't even require me to be there. Clean-up is a snap because there's rarely much left to clean up. What's my secret?

Easy. Simply make a huge sign that says everything is free. I kid you not. It's the answer to every rummage-sale nightmare and also the perfect solution to cleaning out your garage, closets, attic, basement and shed.

I had my first "Everything's Free" rummage sale on a beautiful seventy-degree August day. As I dropped a bag of garbage in the trash can in the garage, I looked around and decided to get organized—which, in reality, meant I had to get rid of a mountain of junk that had taken root on the ceiling-to-floor shelves that lined one whole wall of my garage. Noting that most of it wasn't really worth much in terms of good American dollars, I decided on the spot to just give it all away.

Within five minutes my teenage son had set up a great big sawhorse table for me next to the street. Then I just started handing him stuff to carry out there to set on the table and on the ground all around the table. Huge planters, old throw rugs, garbage cans, plants, books, purses, shoes, shirts, baseball caps, even a huge, never-used crisper like they use in Florida to keep crackers and potato chips moisture-free. There was a well-worn mattress cover, an old torn comforter, bike fenders, a cracked butter dish, ancient plant food, plastic buckets and more gadgets and gizmos than one person should be allowed to accumulate in a lifetime.

I found a giant piece of cardboard that I'd saved to put under the car to catch leaking oil and took a can of spray paint to it. Five minutes later, bright green sixteen-inch-tall letters proclaimed that one word: FREE. But oh, what a wallop that one word packs.

While I was still bringing out stuff to the street, including a dozen empty cardboard boxes (in case someone was moving and needed them) a gentleman pulled up in a van and started loading some of my castoffs into the back end of his car.

"Just put my wife and daughters on a plane to Mexico," he beamed.

"She's gonna kill you for bringing home all this junk," I laughed.

The man beamed. "Oh no, this is good stuff."

I just shook my head and walked back in the house.

I went into my home office to begin my work for the day but every forty-five minutes or so I'd look out the front door to see if any of my worse-than-junk collection was disappearing. By 2:00 PM two-thirds of it was gone.

The next day, after adding lots more stuff to the "free" sale from inside my house, I was on Wisconsin's Lake Nagawicka having lunch on a houseboat with four friends while my best-idea-ever rummage sale was going full blast, with no help from me or anyone, except those customers who were enjoying their "all sales final" free shopping spree. When I got home the only things left were one shoe that had no mate to begin with, an ugly purse that Goodwill probably would have rejected and a beat-up old metal garbage can with a hole in the bottom.

I figure most of those people who helped themselves to my freebies must have needed those things. Or even if they just wanted them because it made them happy to get something for nothing, I know the feelings that stirred within me were much more powerful and satisfying than anything anybody felt who took my stuff. Not only was it just plain delightful to give without any thought of getting anything in return, but, with very little work, my entire garage was cleaned out and my collection of clutter and claptrap from inside the house was eliminated.

I enjoyed that rummage sale so much that I did it every year until I pared down my almost-sixty-years worth of collections to the point where I was able to move to a small condo without suffering anaphylactic shock from trying to cram a gallon's worth of stuff into a quart jar.

Just think, if everybody had free rummage sales, parents of older children could share the baby clothes and toddler toys with young couples who really need the stuff. Older couples could get rid of their sixty- and seventy-year's-worth of collecting without a hassle. New homeowners could have the rakes and lawn equipment not needed by those moving to condos.

Second Corinthians 9:7–8 says it best: "Don't force anyone to give more than he really wants to, for cheerful givers are the ones God prizes. God is able to make it up to you by giving you everything you need and more, so that there will not only be enough for your own needs, but plenty left over to give joyfully to others." (TLB)

And that, my friend, is exactly why I believe that money is definitely not one of the five things we need to be happy. Life is just so much simpler, with less stress, worry and irritation when you're not spending your time fretting about the old stuff you have and the new stuff you want. Who needs all that stuff anyway?

Life's Too Short to Fret about Money

Two things let me live comfortably with a below-poverty income during the years I was raising my children: In 1989, I paid off my house, so I had no rent or house payments, just three hundred dollars a month in property taxes. And for nine years, from 1989 through 1997, my youngest son Andrew received social security payments because his father died when he was nine years old. That helped considerably with child-rearing costs.

Other than those two assists, I had the usual dilemmas of any low-income person. But somehow I managed to help my children get through college. They also helped themselves with loans, scholarships, work-study programs and various part-time jobs.

In general, I've had a great life living on twelve to twenty grand a year. If you're thinking about quitting that back-and-mind-bustin' job and doing something you really love for, say, a thousand or maybe two thousand bucks a month, here are nineteen money-savers that helped me make it work. Maybe they'll give you some ideas so you can become one of us—one of the financially poor, but rich-in-blessings happy people.

1 If you have an extra bedroom or two, open your home and your life and rent those rooms out. You'll not only make money, it'll end loneliness forever. I used the extra bedrooms and bathroom in my house as a boarding house for airline pilots who were based in Milwaukee but lived elsewhere. The pilots donated to my property-taxes-and-utilities fund in exchange for being able to stay at my house whenever they had to be in town. The fun and laughter I had during those ten years more than made up for the loss of privacy. In fact, many of the young men

who stayed at my house became good friends and were super role models for Andrew, the only child still living at home during that time. We even got to know the pilots' wives and children, and the arrangement made us all winners.

2 I purchased a new-but-inexpensive car in 1987 and drove it for seventeen years until I moved to Florida. I took good care of that car and got 193,000 miles out of her. Old Red got regular oil changes, check-ups at the car doctor and once every five years, a new set of tires. I was very proud of that little red Toyota wagon. So proud that when I moved to Florida, I purchased another red Toyota, a used one for only two thousand dollars. This one is six years newer, a sporty little Paseo with a CD player, air-conditioning that works and a sun roof. Believe me, you don't need a sixty thousand dollar car to make you happy.

3 Over the years I learned that for household necessities, furniture, tools, sports items and toys for children and grandchildren, neighborhood rummage, garage and estate sales are a great place to shop. My house in Wisconsin was full of rummage-sale treasures. Sometimes at rummage sales you can even find new gifts like silver and crystal, still in their original boxes, never used, for about ten cents on the dollar. They make great economical presents for friends and relatives.

4 Convinced that many people in this country are addicted to shopping, on September 1, 1995, I made a serious promise to myself not to buy any clothes for three years. I did it because I had two closets full of clothing, and when I quit my job to stay home and write I didn't need dress-up or office work clothes any more. Do you know how long it takes to wear out a jogging suit? Forever-and-a-day just begins to describe how long. And since knit things with elastic waists became my basic work wardrobe

when I started working at home, I figured it would take me at least four years to wear out all the clothes I'd accumulated over the years. Not buying clothes was a tremendous way to save money. The longer I did without clothes shopping, the richer I felt. Not only that, but during the three years and four months that I didn't buy any clothes (except underwear and shoes) I developed a real hatred of shopping that's still with me today.

During those years my friends and relatives took delight in buying me clothes for my birthday or Christmas. Or they would give me their hand-me-downs. My friend Gail gave me a terrific blouse she bought at a rummage sale. Heidi gave me a dress she'd outgrown that I wore to a book signing. Later she sent me a whole box of her clothes that she'd grown tired of. But they were all new to me. Elvi, my friend in Germany, gave me an expensive pair of jeans. From September 1995 through December 1998, I didn't spend a penny on clothes. Staying away from the malls and department stores freed me to do things I truly enjoyed.

5 I buy bulk food and make double and triple batches when I cook so I can freeze much of it for use later on. Buying and cooking in bulk not only saves money, it saves cooking time as well. Another way I save money in the food department is by buying very little meat—some fish and chicken, but not very much red meat. Rice, beans, pasta, lentils, fresh fruits and vegetables, as we all know, are much healthier eating anyway and are certainly less expensive. I often bake my own bread in a bread machine. Talk about a happy activity—the aroma alone of fresh baked bread is worth the price of the miracle machine that does all the work. I also make my own granola and oatmeal mixtures and both, if I may say so myself, are delicious—and very economical.

6 Instead of feeling guilty because I can't contribute lots of money to my church, I donate my time and talent instead. Teaching religious education classes, organizing a nursery or a singles group is probably more valuable to the well-being of a church family than the extra money anyway.

7 When my children were still at home I shopped the sales for all their clothes. In fact, even when I was still buying clothes for myself, I don't think I ever once bought anything that wasn't on sale. I recently purchased a nice twenty-eight dollar shirt for Andrew for five dollars. It had been marked down three or four times before I scooped it up. (Of course, if it's teenagers you're buying for, it's always a good idea to bring them along because their tastes and ours meld about once every third Sunday in a month that starts with *F*.) When the children were little I found great bargains on excellent quality fashions at rummage sales, but that tactic usually only works for preschoolers who don't yet have their own finely tuned sense of style and fashion.

8 When I'm looking for things to furnish my home office, I visit unusual places to find bargains. When the local prison had a sale on surplus office equipment I jumped at the opportunity. A very nice young man in an orange jumpsuit helped carry my dandy office table to the car and then placed my five-dollar bill in the money box as full payment. Instead of buying five hundred sheets of paper at a time for my printer, I buy five thousand at a great discount at the local warehouse outlet store.

9 I try not to make many long distance calls unless it's on my cell phone during "free nights and weekends" time. If someone gives me an 800 number, I use it.

10 As we all know, a healthy body and mind eliminate the need for spending atrocious amounts of money on medical care. So I eat healthy, exercise and try to live as stress-free as I possibly can. That way my relatively inexpensive medical insurance, with its high deductible, is all I need. If disaster strikes and I have huge hospital bills, I'll pay them off one hundred dollars a month for life if necessary.

11 Most states have a program that provides free mammograms for women with low incomes. In Wisconsin, where I lived for twenty-four years, it's called the Wisconsin Women's Cancer Control Program, and all one has to do is visit the local health department to fill out the form for a free mammogram every year. The children and I also took advantage of the free immunizations that the health department offers.

12 Why is it that gift-giving so often turns into a megamerchandising, out-of-control, who-can-buy-the-most-expensive-gift event? Why do people think they have to spend so much money on gifts for friends, family, coworkers, or employees? The only people I exchange gifts with at Christmas are my children and grandchildren. My folks, siblings and most of my friends realized long ago that expensive gifts at holiday time or birthday time or whatever time simply aren't necessary to preserve our friendship. Besides, I've learned over the years that a gift I've made myself or a photo album of a special trip we took together is much more appreciated than an expensive item from a department store.

13 Remember the airline pilots who used my house as their home away from home? Well, those pilots and other friends and relatives in the airline industry allowed me to travel inexpensively with "friend passes" that often only cost fifteen percent of full-fare tickets. When I visited friends all over the county and a few in Europe, I encouraged them to visit me when they traveled. That

way we both got free housing when traveling. Visiting people in their homes makes for a much more enjoyable and relaxed time when you're traveling to a strange place than paying big bucks for a cold, impersonal hotel. The food is usually better too.

14 "Save first, buy later" is my motto. Not the "buy now, pay later" mentality that the credit-card companies would like you to adopt. My system keeps all that interest money in my own pocket. My system gives me a great sense of satisfaction that my treasure is paid for in full, rather than worrying if I'll have enough to cover this month's credit card bill. I have never paid interest on a charge card, nor have I ever borrowed money for household items. I even paid cash for my new car in 1987 and thus saved lots of money on interest. And it, by the way, was the only car I will ever buy new. A two- or three-year-old car can be had for a fraction of the cost of a new one. You know what they say, "That first trip around the block with a new car usually costs you a couple of thousand dollars, minimum." Buy a can of "New Car Smell" and spray it all over the interior if that's what you want, but don't waste your money on a brand new car.

15 I never did believe that it was my duty to buy expensive things for my children. They never had CD players, top-of-the-line stereo equipment, expensive bikes, cars or clothes with brand-name labels on them while they were living at home. Instead of working overtime or extra hours to buy those things, I was home with them, supervising homework, playing games, popping popcorn, driving them to their activities, getting to know their friends, monitoring their TV watching or just hanging around being Mom. I think they'll always be glad they had a mom who wasn't caught up in the "I have to work overtime to buy you things" rat race.

16 When it comes to entertainment, I look for bargains on tickets and special events. If you can get into a festival with a canned good between 10:00 AM and noon, I'm there at 11:30 AM with a can of corn in my pocket. I only watch movies at the budget theaters if I can help it. When my kids were growing up there was a theater a few miles from my home with eight screens that charged a dollar per show all day Tuesdays and Fridays before 5:30 PM. All the rest of the time they were only $1.99 each. Why spend ten dollars to see a film when, if you just wait a month or two, it's at the inexpensive theater? Also, if you usher at live performances, you can get in free. And many plays and concerts have reduced ticket prices for previews or the dress rehearsal on the night before opening night.

17 By the time my youngest finished college I'd had children in college full-time for seventeen years in a row. And for four of those years I had three in college at once. How did a single parent with a poverty-level income manage that? Easily. In fact, I think it's easier for a single parent with a low income to get her children though college than it is for a dual-income, two-parent family. Children in low-income families get loans, grants, scholarships, work-study programs and part-time jobs. Every campus has hundreds of jobs available to students. No parent needs to feel a hundred-percent responsible for providing their children's' college educations. In fact, because my kids had to work so hard for theirs, I think they studied more and worked harder to get good grades than those whose parents handed it to them as a gift they didn't have to earn.

18 Don't be afraid to ask your family, neighbor or friends to help you with such household things as plumbing repairs or minor repair and improvement on the house, yard or car. I've often asked friends and neighbors how to do specific fix-it jobs. Or sometimes, I'd just ask if they'd teach me how to do it. The work not only gets done during the teaching but I learn a valuable new skill as well.

19 Since I'm not a shopper, I rarely buy personal things for myself like make-up, clothes, perfume or jewelry. I wear little or no makeup and usually only get three professional haircuts a year. I do my own nails and hair and don't own any "dry clean only" clothes. It all adds up to one thing: Less stress and more time to really *live* happily.

Does money buy happiness? No. A simple, less stress-filled life and time to enjoy it provide happiness.

It may sound hokey, but it's true. The best things in life really are free: Time with your children. A walk in the woods. A splash in the lake. A phone call to a friend. A visit with Aunt Eva. Watching the sun rise or set with a young child or your favorite house guest. A letter from a pen pal. A free summer concert in the park. A good book from the library. Getting together with friends. A whole day with a best friend. A game of Chinese checkers with a spouse.

I'm still in the poverty-level range income-wise, but I count my riches in interesting friendships, happy relationships and the freedom to spend my life exactly the way I want. If a long walk in the morning with a friend is part of my day, I don't feel guilty that I'm not at my computer working. I treasure those moments because they're more valuable than cash in the bank. Life is for living, not for padding the bank account.

Excuse me, I'm going for a swim. The glorious Gulf of Mexico is just a short bike ride from my condo. I'll work on the next chapter tomorrow.

The Budget

My take on this whole money thing is due partly to the fact that my parents didn't have much money to speak of and yet as a child, I felt we were the richest people I knew. My mother kept the household books balanced to the penny. Every month she paid the bills by check—things like the house payment, taxes, insurance, utilities and groceries. The rest of the family income each month was placed in eleven separate envelopes Mother kept in the top drawer of her bookkeeping desk in the living room. The envelopes were labeled Church, School Expenses, Clothes, Gifts, Repair and Improvement, Dues and Licenses, Doctor-Dentist, Savings, Dad's Allowance, Mom's Allowance and Pat's Allowance.

After Mother died in 1979, Dad gave me a box of papers from her desk. Included were her itemized statements for each payday. The June 3, 1960, ledger states that the checks she wrote that month including utilities and the house payment totaled $274. The cash in the envelopes totaled $130. Our family of five was living on $504 a month.

In spite of the tight budget Mother and Dad still gave twenty-four dollars a month to the church. Twenty-four dollars! That was four dollars more than the combined allowance they allotted themselves each month. How many of us would give twenty-four dollars to the church when all we'd have left for ourselves for the entire month would be ten dollars?

As a child I never had the slightest notion that my parents inched their way through such a tight budget every month. We had everything we needed and more: a beautiful home that my dad built, plenty of food (much of it from the big garden out back), nice clothes (so what if most of them were hand-me-downs?), a car, even a family vacation now and then. But every month my mother took out ten dollars for herself, ten dollars for Dad and twenty-four dollars for the church.

I wonder about people who tithe. They're convinced that the more they give, the more it comes back to them. They believe that the Lord provides everything they need when they need it. Now that I think back on my life as a single parent, I have to admit that every time my purse strings were worn to the point of disappearing altogether, I put my basic faith into action and somehow some amazing windfall would plop into my lap, often just enough to carry me through to the next pay period.

Perhaps it's because math was my least favorite subject, but I've never balanced my checkbook in my life. I subtract the checks I write but at the end of the month I never try to balance my figures with the bank's. It cost me a date once—a blind date who worked in a bank and balanced his checkbook to the penny every month, and was aghast that I didn't. He never called back. Somehow I think that's a good thing.

I just hope that if there's ever a mistake in the bank's favor that someday there will be one in mine. It's about having other, more important or more interesting things to do with my life than sit in a corner like Mr. Scrooge counting my money. There are simply too many people to love, too much living to be done, too much to hope for, so much faith to rely on and too much laughter to worry about money. And that's why I don't think money is all that it's cracked up to be and why it's certainly not one of the major ingredients for happiness.

Chapter Two

Someone to Love

Love doesn't make the world go round.
Love is what makes the ride worthwhile.
—*Franklin P. Jones*

The first ingredient to happiness is someone to love. Notice I didn't say, "someone to love me," or "someone to love you." No, I said, "someone to love."

I'm blessed with so many people to love that it's no wonder I'm happy every day of my life. An amazing dad and stepmom head the list because they're the oldest and deserve the most respect. Dad and Bev have been married since 1982. (Mother died in 1979.) I have four incredible children, Jeanne, Julia, Michael and Andrew. I think the fact that I dragged them through two marriages and two divorces makes me love them all the more because they survived and they're all smart, interesting and talented. They have spouses and they all have children. So here's how they go together: Jeanne and Canyon and Adeline, born in 2004; Julia and her three: Hailey born in 1993, Casey, 1998 and Riley, 2000; Michael and Amy and their three redheads: Hannah, 1996, Zachary, 1998, Chloe, 2002; Andrew and Carrissa and Ethan, born in 2005.

I have one brother, Joe, and one sister-in-law, Linda; one sister, Catherine, and one brother-in-law, Bill; three nieces; one nephew; dozens of cousins; two aunts left out of twelve aunts and uncles. It's a nice family. We're scattered all over the United States, but when we get together we love every minute of it. And like I said, I'm aware every day of my life of how much I love these people.

It's the act of loving someone else that's essential—whether it's a husband or wife, children, grandchildren, friends, relatives, a girlfriend or boyfriend, a teacher, neighbors or coworkers. Even the love you have for a dog, a cat or any dear pet is enough to jumpstart your happiness buttons.

The interesting thing about loving someone is that it usually produces a boomerang effect: The love we give is almost always returned to us. But it's the act of loving others that is the most important part of this key to happiness. It's simply loving someone, nourishing that love, giving him or her your time, energy and devotion. It doesn't have to be boy-meets-girl, ka-ching, ka-chang, wheeeee, fall in love, bells, whistles, wedding, kids, college bills, empty nest and now-let's-see-if-we-still-like-each-other-enough-to-stay-in-this-thing-until-death-do-us-part.

No, having someone to love is easier than all that. Just find someone—anyone—spouse, child, parent, other relative, friend, neighbor, teacher, someone—anyone—to love. I'm going to say it again in case you blinked the last time. It's the act of loving someone else that makes us happy. It's true, more often than not, that when we do love someone that person usually loves us back and we get all kinds of bonuses from that. But the loving-us-back isn't the important part of the happiness equation. It's the act of loving someone else that makes us happy.

Root Beer Floats and Other Notes

We hear a lot about self-esteem these days, how important it is in the development of a child's personality . . . and how easy it is to destroy it with a few thoughtless words.

When I was growing up in the 1950s, my parents didn't know much about self-esteem. They were just parents—hardworking, God-fearing, good people who didn't read psychology books or get bogged down with self-help articles. They raised two daughters and one son. I was the oldest (nine years older than my brother, thirteen years older than my sister) and there was never a doubt in their minds as to whether or not I would grow up to be a happy, reasonably successful woman.

Even though my dad worked as a rural mail carrier and Mother balanced their small household budget to the penny each month, conversations were never prefaced with, "Girls don't need to go to college," or "*If* we can afford to send you to college. . . ." Instead, from the time I was in grade school I can remember exciting conversations that began with, "*When* you go to college . . . ."

My parents expected us to have good educations, careers, raise families, be successful. But most of all they wanted us to be happy with our lives. Their "just do it" vision and "work for it yourself" plan succeeded. All three of us are college graduates. My brother Joe is a 747 airline pilot. My sister Catherine is a first-grade teacher. We all have a boatload of self-esteem—one quality I will always say is a direct gift from my parents.

Building self-esteem somehow came naturally to Mom and Dad. I remember one event in particular during my childhood as clearly as if it happened yesterday. To this day I believe it had more to do with building my self-esteem than anything anyone has ever said or done for me before or since.

It was a simple thing, really, but honestly, it was my first glimpse into what it truly means to love someone else. I saw, firsthand, my folks loving me. *Me!* It happened one Saturday night when I was about six or seven years old. I'd gone to bed at my usual time, eight or eight-thirty. By 9:00 PM I was into a sound sleep when I felt a hand on my shoulder.

"Pat, wake up," Dad whispered as he shook me gently. "Are you awake? Your mother and I want you to come out to the kitchen."

"Huh? Why, Daddy?"

"Well, we decided to have root beer floats and we don't want you to miss out. Come on, honey, there's a big 'brown cow' out there for you."

Wide-eyed and astounded, I slipped on my blue-flannel bathrobe and my big pink fluffy slippers and padded to the kitchen. I plopped down next to Mom at the old wooden table. I watched Dad scoop the vanilla ice cream into the large blue, yellow and brown stoneware mugs, only used on special occasions because they were treasures from my mother's childhood.

The foam from the root beer tickled my nose as I chatted with my folks about school. Then I listened excitedly as Mom and Dad discussed plans for our family vacation. They even asked my opinion about the things I wanted to do on our camping trip. Mom said I could go to the Piggly-Wiggly with her and pick out my very own bag of candy to take on the trip.

"Need some more root beer on that ice cream, honey?" Daddy asked as he created a new mound of delicious suds in my mug.

I never felt more loved than I did that night in the kitchen as I groggily slurped root beer and ice cream with my parents. Why?

Because Mom and Dad wanted my company enough to wake me up so I could be there. Me! Just a kid! Wow, what a glorious feeling!

The best part was seeing how happy it made my folks to love me. Mom and Dad were loving me, not just with words, but with actions that sunk in, even at age six. I could actually feel how loving me made them happy. After all, they loved me enough to wake me up so I could be a part of their root beer float event. And as all parents know, getting your little treasures into bed and asleep in the first place is often harder than working an eight-hour shift during the day. And once you do get the kids into bed, the last thing a normal parent is going to do is wake them up before morning.

I don't know if I understood then what it meant to really, truly love someone, but on that evening I figured out that they loved me, without a doubt, and I knew their love for me made them happy.

Tea Time with Dad

My father was the Rural Route Two mail carrier in my hometown of Rock Falls, Illinois, for more than thirty years. Every morning from Monday to Saturday he'd get up at 5:00 AM, go to the post office, sort the mail, then pack it into his car around nine o'clock and deliver it to his five hundred patrons scattered up and down more than fifty miles of blacktop and gravel roads.

Since our house, the house he built right after World War II, the house he still lives in today, was between the post office and the start of his route, Dad would stop at home for a quick breakfast before heading out to deliver the mail. In the years before my brother and sister were born, Dad's morning ritual sometimes included tea with me in my bedroom.

I was only four, five and six years old during those tea parties but I remember them clearly. First the begging: "Daddy, please, please come back to my room for a tea party before you leave."

"Okay, I'll be back as soon as I finish having breakfast with your mother."

I'd scurry off to my room to make the preparations. Mother had given me her childhood set of mint-green depression glass child's dishes: two cups, two saucers, two four-inch-in-diameter sandwich plates, a creamer and sugar bowl. No teapot—no problem. I'd already learned that pouring tea with a pretend teapot is fine as long as you have real cups to pour it into.

I'd scoot my desk chair into the middle of my bedroom for Dad and I'd straddle the lower end of a combination table/bookcase that Dad had made for my knickknacks. The top part of that little table was the perfect place for the tea dishes.

After I poured the pretend tea and set the pretend cakes and pretend tea sandwiches on the two sandwich plates, I'd pick up my tiny teacup and blow on it to cool the steaming pretend tea. Then I'd settle back and ask Dad a question.

"So, what's new, Daddy?"

I don't remember all his answers to my many questions or even his questions and my answers. I do remember talking about our big family garden. Usually he'd remind me to help Mom pick raspberries that morning. Sometimes we talked about my turtles out in "Pat's Turtle Ranch," the words he'd carved into the concrete he'd poured around an old tractor tire as a home for my growing collection of turtles.

On those tea party mornings Dad listened more than he talked as I prattled on about my best friend Vivian who lived up the hill next door to us. Some mornings I hauled out my dress-up clothes and paraded around my room as a fancy-dancing queen or an elegant lady for his enjoyment.

Dad may have even brought the newspaper with him into my bedroom on a few occasions while we sipped pretend tea together. It doesn't matter what we talked about, did or thought during those tea parties. What matters is that for fifteen minutes during his busy, "Have to go to work now, Honey" mornings, my Dad took the time to have tea with his daughter. The tea wasn't real. The sandwiches, cookies and cakes weren't real. But the love I felt from my Dad sure was. And to this day, I still love a good tea party, with real tea, of course, especially when Dad's around to enjoy it with me.

Is there a child or grandchild in your life who could use a boost of self-esteem? The best doses come when you simply let that child know, without a doubt, that you really, truly want to *be* with them and that you treasure them enough to share your most precious moments with them in person. It's all about the gift of your time, the best gift anyone can give to a child, the gift that truly defines *someone to love.*

The Swell SWILL Sisters

What happens when you don't have a spouse and all your relatives live in other states? Whom do you find to love? My second husband Harold left me for an older woman. Yikes, it's bad enough when they leave you for a younger woman . . . but an older one? Oh my poor psyche! He married her the day of our divorce and then died two years later. Somewhere during those two years I'd come to grips with the fact that I didn't have a man in my life, a man who loved me unconditionally.

In 1989, the year my second husband died, I decided to do something about the wrenching loneliness that permeated my life, even though I had two kids in college, one in high school and one in grade school. Most of my friends were happily married couples who pretty much socialized with each other and didn't include a place at their dinner tables for a third wheel.

However, I got the ball rolling in my "someone to love" quest that year because of an odd phone call from a woman I'd never met. There I was, sitting in the old green rocker in my family room one Friday night minding my own business, which probably involved watching an old movie or a sitcom rerun on TV, when the phone rang.

The stranger on the other end was a woman named Sunny calling from Valdosta, Georgia. Seems she'd read an article I'd written for a single-parent magazine, and she wanted to share some of the miseries of her own single-parenting experiences with me. She talked for an hour. I listened and nodded. I even said, "Uh-huh," once in a while. When she was finished telling me every detail of her two divorces, the life histories of her two daughters, one from each husband, and the miseries of trying to find meaningful work down South, I was exhausted just from listening. Like me, Sunny was from northern Illinois originally, but she felt like an ear of corn planted in a cotton field and really hated the Deep South. She asked if she could call me back the following week.

I said, "Sure. It's your nickel." I never was good at quick thinking.

And she did.

She called me every Friday night for weeks. I started to open up and tell her a little about my life as a single parent of four—three teens and a nine-year-old whose father, my ex-husband Harold, was dying of leukemia. I was still a tad bitter about the fact that he'd married the other woman, and I was still angry, hurt and feeling overwhelmed with my single-parent responsibilities.

As the months went by Sunny grew more and more interested in leaving the South, even if only for a long weekend. I suggested she come to Milwaukee to attend SingleFest, a huge event sponsored by the University of Wisconsin. It would be two busy days, with lots of classes, dinners, dances and the possibility of meeting other interesting single people. I even invited her to stay at my house for the weekend.

She came, stayed for an entire week and bought a house five miles from my own while she was here. The following August she moved herself and her two young daughters up to my section of the country—into my life, my psyche and my free time.

Sunny wanted me to be her new best friend. I was, after all, the only person she knew in the entire state of Wisconsin.

Well now, if that wasn't the worst predicament I'd ever found myself in, it was because that particular year turned out to be the lousiest year of my life. I was in a bad mood practically all year. It was the year the man I'd been dating for eight months suddenly left town and moved clean out of state without telling me. He was a relocated government witness, a Mafia wannabe in his earlier years. I'm telling you, I was definitely standing in the wrong line when God passed out the husband-hunting genes.

John and I were writing a book about his life of crime. Talk about a working relationship that could spice up the life of a single parent of four who wrote radio commercials for a living! John was an uneducated, short, skinny little thing and I was always on the verge of trying to lose forty pounds, but nevertheless, we seemed to hit it off. When I look back on our eight months of dating, I think he was attracted to my ability to write a decent story, and I was attracted to the fact that he was a man who seemed remotely interested in me—or was he just interested in having me help him write his memoirs? At any rate, the FBI and the federal marshals suddenly decided John would be safer living in another city, so he disappeared one day. He called me later from Tulsa, Oklahoma, and told me he was in nursing school. This from a man who once shot the kneecaps off a guy in a bar.

Then, a few months later, my oldest daughter Jeanne was caught smack-dab in the middle of a California earthquake. This was the one that buckled bridges, destroyed buildings and generally shook up the entire San Francisco Bay area for months. Jeanne was working in a bookstore at the time. She rushed through the aisles trying to get the customers out of the store because books were flying everywhere. As soon as she rounded them all up and ushered them outside, the street in front of them buckled and separated right in front of their eyes. It was a traumatic time for my daughter. But for a mother fearing the worst and not being able to get in touch because of downed power lines, it enhanced a year long bad mood considerably.

Two months after that, my ex-husband died, much to the horror and angst of my youngest child, Andrew. Try taking a nine-year-old through the death of his father, knowing you had to do everything humanly possibly to ease your child's pain, while at the same time trying to control your anger over the fact that the man who'd died had left you two years earlier for another woman—the *older* woman, remember?

Yes, 1989 was a bad year. I wallowed in misery, pain, grief, loneliness, fear and bitterness from March through December. And right in the middle of it, Sunny moved to Milwaukee and gave me the title, New Best Friend.

Only God Himself knows how much I did not feel like being anyone's best friend that year. I wanted to crawl into that bat cave and let ten thousand batwings lull me to sleep. I was too busy organizing my pity party day after day as I struggled to get up and go to work every morning in the midst of worrying about whether or not Jeanne was safe, wondering if John would ever come back to me, and now desperately trying to ease the pain my fourth and youngest child was experiencing because of the death of his father.

But Sunny kept calling. "Let's go out for dinner tonight." Or, "Why don't you and Michael and Andrew come over for dinner?" Both of my daughters were away at college. Michael was a senior in high school, busy with the marching band and dating his beloved Amy, and Andrew was in third grade. The last place on earth my two boys wanted to be was at Sunny's house on a school night with her two preschool-age daughters.

"I can't. Michael has a game tonight." Or, "I really have a lot of work to do." I really had no work to do. My writing well had dried up. I simply didn't feel like being her best friend.

Finally, after she had talked me into one too many events that included her two daughters, I decided I had to find some friends for Sunny—friends who would keep her entertained, friends who had younger children who would find her kids fascinating.

I decided a Friday night would be a good night to gather all the women I knew, bring them into my home and hope like the dickens that a few of them would take over my role as Sunny's best friend. I invited every friend I'd made in the nine years I'd lived in Wisconsin. I invited women from the neighborhood. Women from church, from work and the writer's group I belonged to. I invited the mothers of my children's friends.

Twenty-seven women gathered in my family room that evening, including Sunny and myself. After they all arrived I nearly worked myself into a panic. *These women don't know each other,* I thought. *What if they just sit there?* I had no plans or agenda for the evening, just a bunch of snack foods and a family room full of women, most of whom had never been in my home before.

I shouldn't have worried. I have since learned that when you put even two or three women who are strangers in a room together, it takes about two minutes before they're talking up a storm, sharing bits of their lives, problems, concerns, adventures, goals and plans. I've also figured out, in the years since, that it generally takes men about two years of friendship before they get off sports and start talking about themselves or their lives.

So there I was, eight or ten different conversations going on all around me. I jumped from group to group, fearing I'd miss one word of the most interesting conversations I'd ever heard. Wow! I had no idea that Barb felt pinned in by the fact that two of her sons had recently moved back into her house after leaving for school and the army. I was surprised to learn that Tina was thinking of leaving her executive job because of personality conflicts at work. Gail shared that more than anything she wanted to go back to college and get a degree in nursing now that her own two were in college. Betsy made us all laugh with antics of her new first-grade class.

I introduced everyone to Sunny, then crossed my fingers that most of them would call her and plan things that didn't include me. I poured drinks, offered plates of cookies and candy—chocolate, lots of chocolate.

Sunny stood up and quieted the room, tossed back her long mane of shiny thick brown wavy hair and said in her best Southern voice, "You know, down South they referred to us women as *precious*. Ya'll aren't just precious. You're downright interesting!"

Tina laughed, stood up, threw her arms into the air and said, 'You know what? We *are* interesting! Every one of us. Interesting women with interesting careers and families and dreams and problems. Even our problems are interesting."

The women laughed and applauded. Someone else echoed

Tina's words about how we were the most interesting women she'd ever met.

Tina continued, "Yes! I think all of us in this room tonight should form a group and call it the Southeastern Wisconsin Interesting Ladies League. I think we should meet right here in Pat's family room once a month on the first Friday of the month. After all, she doesn't have a husband to uproot. We can all bring snacks so she doesn't have to do that all by herself."

"Meet here once a month?" I could barely get the words out. I repeated the woman's suggested name for the group slowly, "Southeastern Wisconsin Interesting Ladies League—S-W-I-L-L. You want to form a group and call it SWILL?" I hoped the name alone would persuade her to change her mind.

"Yes! That's a great idea," one woman sitting near the wood burner said.

"Yeah, we can talk about the swill in our lives as well as all the good stuff. It'll be cathartic and refreshing," bubbled Diane.

"Sure, I could easily make it on the first Friday of every month," another chirped.

"Let's keep it simple. No dues, no officers, no rules," Eunice beamed.

"Yes, a woman's group with no committees and no fund-raisers!" from Anita, who was practically giggling with enthusiasm.

"No bylaws, no minutes! We'll just come and talk and share and maybe solve a few problems for each other," Barb offered.

Oh, they were on a roll now. I was still sputtering, trying to say something like, *But, don't you get it? This whole thing was for one purpose only, to find some friends for Sunny. A one-time event. My job was supposed to be finished after tonight.*

But I couldn't get the words out. Everyone else was talking too fast—a roomful of excited women, all of whom were acting like they'd just met their new best friends. Almost as if they'd been starved for additional "someones to love" for decades.

"No dress code. We'll come in our most casual clothes so we can *be* comfortable. And from now on, when we gather, let's take turns talking so everyone can hear what everyone else has to say," Jody suggested.

Jean, a wise practicing psychologist in her seventies, advised that whatever would be shared in my large family room, should stay in the room. "That way, everyone will feel freer to share what's really on her mind."

As I looked around the room, I saw women of all ages, all religions, all economic backgrounds, different nationalities. Some happily married, some divorced, a few never married, one widow. Mothers with young children, others with teenagers. A few grandmothers. All animated, chatting, sharing, opening up. My heart softened and in a weak moment I said, "Yes."

SWILL lasted sixteen years, until I moved from Wisconsin to Florida in the fall of 2004. Every single SWILL meeting was at my house—gladly, on my part, because I made a few rules for myself. I never cleaned my house before a SWILL meeting, and I didn't make or buy fancy refreshments. A bag of pretzels and maybe a bag of red licorice and a couple of two-liter soda bottles were all I contributed. Sometimes women brought snack foods, once in a while someone would bring a fancy leftover dessert from home. If one of the women was having a chocolate or salty foods craving, she'd bring a bag of candy or chips and toss it on the coffee table.

I learned years ago that many women's groups disband after a few years because they get to be get fixated on who can make the highest lemon meringue pie or use the fanciest china or most elegant silver service. SWILL was a sort of paper-napkin, paper-plate, leftovers-are-fine kind of group, and it worked. And for sixteen years, until I moved, I was happy to host it.

We never lost sight of the fact that the important thing about SWILL was that the women were the key elements, not the food or the house decorations. As the years passed and life seemed to be busier and busier for many of the women, we started skipping the summer months. Then we decided not to meet in December because of all the holiday parties and preparations. Eventually, SWILL met regularly five times a year, in January, March, May, September and November. And after all those years SWILL still had no dues, no minutes, no committees, no rules, no dress code, no food assignments, no bylaws, no agenda, no fund-raisers and no purpose. We were simply interesting women from all walks of life who gathered to gab, unwind, discuss, chat, advise, listen, learn, laugh, relax, relate and revitalize.

SWILL was a place to make new friendships and nourish old ones. Sometimes I'd never even met the women who showed up at my door. That was because anyone could bring a friend, and if that friend liked us, she could come forever. This wasn't a group of just my friends. It was for any interesting woman who wanted to join us. All we did was gather around in a circle in my family room and take turns talking so everyone could hear what everyone else had to say.

Sometimes at SWILL we laughed all evening. Sometimes we cried. Usually we heard stories from the deepest parts of each others' hearts. I remember one night in particular when the evening was magical in the diversity of life-altering stories we heard. I've changed the names of the SWILL members to protect their privacy, but their stories are true.

Beth described her years of living homeless with her daughter in a car. One night on the interstate when her car broke down, a man stopped. He took Beth and her daughter to a restaurant, fed them and assured them that their lives would change soon. He said a family would help them get on their feet. Then, poof, the man simply disappeared—vanished. Beth turned to look out the window, and when she looked back he was gone. She wondered if she'd imagined talking to him. But sure enough, a few weeks later a family took Beth and her daughter into their home and supported them until they could make it on their own. That was ten years ago, and today Beth has a good job, a nice apartment and is a remarkable mother to her teenage daughter. Beth still believes in angels.

Annie had come to SWILL for the first time that night, just a few days after having gone through breast cancer surgery, and she was fearfully facing chemo. There were a few other women in the room that evening who had already experienced chemo and who reassured Annie and offered their support. We SWILL sisters shed tears, then shared hugs after Annie bravely told her story, punctuated by the struggles of her messy divorce, single-parenthood, variety of jobs and many moves in recent years.

Grace shared news about her decision to start a new career as a parish nurse after more than thirty years as an emergency room nurse. In the previous year Grace and her retired husband had sold the home where they'd raised their five children and moved to a new, smaller home twenty-five miles away. Leaving her old home and neighborhood was traumatic for Grace, but we SWILL members saw courage and excitement spilling out as she talked about the college courses she was taking that would help her change careers at age sixty.

Amy, a beautiful, blond, forty-something woman who had experienced far too many surgeries and health problems in the previous fifteen years, told us that she'd just met a very interesting man, a golfer like her. She giggled and glowed with the joy of a new friendship as she described the fun she was having with her new gentleman.

Peggy, a strong leader in her church, told us that she was seeking a divorce after thirty years of marriage . . . a divorce, she said, that should have happened five years earlier. "These days, my life is a seesaw of loneliness and fear on the one hand and excitement and anticipation on the other."

When it was Kelly's turn she said, "As I listen to the ups and downs of what's going on in your lives I realize how happy and content I am with my life right now. My job is going great, kids are all healthy, my husband and I are getting along fine. I'm working on my master's degree, and I love my classes. Hearing your stories makes me want to cherish this moment because I know I'll have worse days and perhaps better days, but for now I'm happy with my life."

Trish, a single parent, shared a similar story. After dreaming for fourteen years about meeting a nice man to date and getting married again, she had come full circle and understood just how happy and complete her life was, empty nest and all. "I've learned that I don't need a husband to be happy."

Teresa talked about the emotional breakdown she'd experienced a few years earlier and then described her involvement in a number of volunteer activities, including visiting people dying of cancer in a hospice. Teresa taught us that giving to others as a volunteer is what truly helps cure our own ills.

Joan's love of her life, the man she met many years after a painful divorce, had died suddenly nine months before this particular SWILL meeting. At the previous meeting Joan had cried soulful tears as she shared the story of her three-year romance with her soulmate, stricken suddenly in his fifties by a deadly pneumonia. On this night, however, Joan was vibrant, happy and chatting about how she knew she must move forward, meet new people and be open to new adventures. Within the year she met and married another soulmate and is now living happily ever after.

Betty regaled the SWILL gang with a hilarious account of a two-week vacation-from-hell that made *National Lampoon's Family Vacation* look like a picnic at the beach. Natural disasters, transportation problems, a rockslide in front of the train they were on and the fact that both she and her husband were sick much of the trip all took their toll. Betty said she fully expected cattle rustlers to hijack the train before they finally arrived home totally exhausted.

Later that evening as I put away the cheese spread and dumped the ice cubes, I thought about our SWILL meeting and what I'd learned that night. Simply put it's this: Life is jam-packed with ups and downs, and it takes a group of friends in one room sharing their life stories to help us see that the good often gets better, the bad sometimes gets worse, but more often than not, the average stuff in between is pretty doggone special. I also learned that it's our friends who help us muddle through. Most of all, I was reminded once again that the SWILL gang had given me so many amazing, wonderful women to love and cherish like sisters.

Even though I was the foot-dragging, no-how-no-way-do-I-want-a-woman's-group-meeting-at-my-house kind of person in 1989, I'm amazed to say that I'm actually the person who gained the most from SWILL. All those years that SWILL was in existence, it gave me lots of someones to love. My women friends were cherished beyond measure. Sometimes I only saw them at SWILL, but I knew they were out there. I learned that by opening my home and my heart to them, my life and my happiness blossomed and bore fruit. *Someone to love.* It has a ring to it. It has made all the difference in my life.

How do you go about loving someone? Easy. Make time for them. Make sure they know how much you love and appreciate them. Tell them. Write them notes. Say "I love you" at the end of phone conversations. Organize get-togethers. Open up your home. Tell people to stop in for tea or coffee anytime. Say, "My door's always open" and mean it.

Who knows, you just might find yourself with so many someones to love that you'll be walking around giggling and saying, "I'm so happy! I love my life!" like I do.

Oh, by the way, Sunny only came to SWILL a few times, joined a woman's group in her own neighborhood and then moved to the Chicago area to take a teaching job. I haven't seen or heard from her since 1990.

In 2004, I left Milwaukee and moved to Florida. A few months later I organized FILL, the Florida Interesting Ladies League. This is a lively group of women who don't meet as regularly as SWILL did, but when we do get together we always have fun. So you see, no matter where you live, it's easy to gather interesting people, form a little group and find lots of someones to love.

As the years flew by and new women wove their way in and out of the SWILL and FILL gatherings, I thought a lot about the power of friendship, and the need, especially for women, to have good close friends. One time, in an e-mail, I received one of those "author unknown" bits of syrupy sweet blah-blah that seem to float through cyberspace on a regular basis. But, okay, I admit it, I liked this one. It was a simple little equation about friendship, very simple, but very true. It goes something like this: "Friends are mathematical. They multiply the joy, divide the sorrows, subtract the past, add to tomorrow. Friendship is bigger than the sum of all its parts."

Well, if that isn't a mouthful, I don't know what is. I do know that when it comes to the women I've met at SWILL and FILL, that little equation is very, very true. All those women over the years, and there were probably seventy or eighty who floated in and out of our SWILL gatherings depending on what was going on in their lives, enriched my life in ways that are hard to calculate unless I look at that simple formula. They multiplied the joys in my life by letting me share my joys with the entire group time and again. They helped me divide my sorrows by listening when I blubbered and encouraging me when I was discouraged. They helped me get over things in my past and move forward toward my future with resolve. And their loving friendship, which grew as time moved forward, was a tremendous comfort when I slipped out of my bed alone each morning.

Women talk to convey or gather information, to think out loud as we explore and discover what it is we want to say, to feel better when we're upset about something and to create intimacy. In other words, women need to talk, share, feel and express those feelings with other women who do the same.

"Females, on the other hand, ask very different questions. 'Do we really need someone with a whistle? Is the person with the whistle using it appropriately? Is having the whistle really worth the price you pay to get it?' Most females decide they will train for whistle-blowing positions but once they get them they will use the whistle very sparingly if at all, thereby proving that whistles are not really necessary."

We all need someone to love. But part of that equation for women is someone to talk to, share, be emotional with and explore new ideas and feelings. We women can actually solve problems just by talking about them. For whatever reason, not fully understood by either sex, women, more often than not, don't want their men to actually solve their problems for them. They just want them to listen to their problems. It's hard for men to do that. They are genetically born to be fixers and problem-solvers. This is why it's such a great idea to have a group of women friends as a basis for your "someone to love" in addition to the parents, spouse, children, grandchildren and other family members in your life.

So form your own SWILL gang. If you live somewhere besides Southeastern Wisconsin, you'll have to change the name of the group as I did when I moved to Florida. Unless you live in Southern West Virginia. Or Southwestern Washington. Or Southern Wyoming.

The Buzz and the Hum

Having *SOMEONE TO LOVE* doesn't always mean warm, fuzzy feelings. Sometimes having someone to love means worry, fear, anguish, wishing-you-could-bear-the-pain instead of them, feelings. Loving them takes on a whole new meaning, but it's just as powerful and is just as much a critical ingredient to happiness.

Andrew, my youngest, was in the hospital for eleven days in 1998. The sounds of the hospital still echo in my brain. . . .

Buzz, buzz, buzz... hum, hum, hum. Buzz, buzz, buzz... hum, hum, hum. The sound is rhythmic, never ending. It's a soft sound, pleasant; it reminds me of the ebb and flow of waves crashing into rocks and then quietly returning to sea. But this sound is even softer than that. This sound could be the background for relaxation tapes of the living earth.

This *buzz-hum* is the sound of four fluids being pumped into my son's veins. The buzzing isn't as soothing as the hum, but nevertheless, at times it has the power to lure both of us toward slumber in his hospital room.

This young man is supposed to be careering through his last four weeks of his senior year in high school. He's supposed to be bragging to me about how many hits he got in softball today, writing that last essay for English class, rattling off his list of graduation gift requests or getting the brakes fixed on his motorcycle.

Instead this eighteen-year-old, six foot three skinny drink of water is lying still with three IV poles lined up like soldiers next to his bed pumping antibiotics, steroids, a saline solution and red blood cells into his left arm. Ulcerative colitis eats at his intestines.

Doctors, nurses and lab technicians poke and prod and stick needles and various plastic and metal things into his body. Granted, they do it lovingly and with tremendous compassion, but they still do it.

I watch, wait and do typical Mom things—rub his back, feed him ice chips, chatter about the real world, fluff his pillow, go on clutter patrol in his room and ask enough questions so that I understand what's being done to my youngest child.

For the first three days I'm so calm and serene I amaze myself. During a particularly quiet moment while thumbing through a magazine I read a quote by Senator Sam Ervin: "Religious faith is not a storm cellar to which men and women can flee for refuge from the storms of life. It is, instead, an inner spiritual strength which enables them to face those storms with hope and serenity."

Of course, I say to myself, I am filled with hope and serenity. Otherwise how can I profess to be a woman of faith? Feeling quite smug, I bask in my serenity, proud of my tower-of-strength attitude. I sit quietly, helplessly, simply loving my son with all my heart.

By the end of Day Four my son is cranky. Four days without food or water, punctuated with pain and constant intrusions into his personal space, have left him without any social skills. He's running on two cylinders instead of eight, so he snaps at me, complains about everything, declares that he's sick of visitors and phone calls and in the end reduces me to tears. I'm not such a pillar after all.

That night, still in my son's room, I whimper to Pastor Tom, "What's wrong with me? I'm losing it. Where's my serenity? Doesn't my faith guarantee serenity?"

"Nonsense," he says. "You can't be in the same room with someone eighteen hours a day for four straight days without losing it. Happily married couples can't even do it when they're perfectly healthy. You need to get out of here. Go for a walk. Take care of you for awhile. I'll stay."

I leave, afraid that if I don't I'll burst into loud shaking sobs. I head for my friend Betsy's house where we walk, talk (mostly me blathering about the whole week with all its gruesome details) and finish off the visit with hugs.

Two hours later I'm back in my son's room. Pastor Tom leaves, the last poking, prodding and injections are completed for the day, and once again, I've settled into a chair next to the IV pumps.

Buzz, buzz, buzz. Hum, hum, hum. As I listen I begin to understand more about what it means to love someone unconditionally. I also begin to understand more about faith. I learn that it's there and that it flows like medicine through an IV, sure and steady. Sometimes the love and the faith buzz. Sometimes they hum. For now, the humming lulls me to sleep.

Gifts of Love and Other Treasures

When Andrew was in the hospital, I learned another life-lesson about happiness. This one was a whopper.

First of all, I'd never once had a friend whose child was a hospital patient. In fact, I can only remember visiting a few friends of mine in the hospital, no more than six or so, during my entire life. (Praise God my friends are so healthy!) So when my son was confined for such a long time and requested no visitors and no phone calls, I launched into my mother mode of being the gauntlet that kept them all away.

I stayed with Andrew all day and evening, dashed home at midnight, slept for five or six hours, woke up without an alarm, wrote a daily update on my computer to friends and family who had e-mail access, returned voice-mail messages, and got back to the hospital by 8:00 AM. And since I wasn't experienced in what one does for really sick people, I stumbled around each time someone said, "What can we do to help? Let us know." My stock answer was, "Oh, nothing, just pray for him."

By Day Four, my friends began to come up with ideas on their own. In the days that followed I learned the absolutely best things one can do for someone whose child is in the hospital. I also learned how having someone to love, lots of someones, fills your heart and truly does make happiness come to you even on your darkest days.

During those eleven days Andrew was in the hospital I learned from Rusty, who came over one afternoon with his own lawnmower and mowed my entire yard, front, sides and back. How he ever got through the foot-tall growth in the backyard is beyond me.

I learned from Jean, a practicing psychologist, who met me in the hospital cafeteria on her way home from work with a large chocolate malt and lent me her listening ear for over an hour.

I learned from Sharon and Kay, who whisked me out of Andrew's hospital room when he was sleeping and took me to the cafeteria for lunch.

I learned from Betsy, who showed up on a perfect ten of a day, warm and sunny, and drove me to the park a mile from the hospital, spread a blanket and produced a three-course picnic, including fresh watermelon. It was a God-moment.

I learned from the usually stern, no-nonsense surgeon when he spent an uncharacteristically long half-hour at my son's bedside explaining with great patience, compassion and hand-drawn diagrams why he couldn't do the needed surgery at that time.

I learned from Heather, who put a large bag of fresh strawberries in my refrigerator for late-night or early morning snacking during my days at the hospital.

I learned from Heather and Rusty's five-year-old Hayley, who made me a bright, happy Mother's Day card that was waiting on my kitchen counter at midnight when I returned from the hospital the night before Mother's Day.

I learned from my friends Al and Gloria, who bought me supper three nights in a row while we worked on a business project together in the hospital cafeteria.

I learned from Ken, one of my son's nurses, who taught Andrew meditation for pain relief at one o'clock in the morning when Andrew couldn't sleep and Ken was on a break from his shift in the emergency room three floors below.

I learned from Kay, who made 232 copies of the handouts I needed for a class I had to teach the next night.

I learned from my pastor, Father Tom, who not only spent hours with Andrew every single day he was in the hospital (the only visitor Andrew wanted besides me), but who also stayed with my son in our home the night he was released and I had to teach.

I learned that I will never ever again do the usual, common things one does when a friend or a friend's child is in the hospital. No, I'll choose from the above, from the list of the most creative, most helpful gifts imaginable. God-moments, every one of them.

Someone to love. I fell in love with them all, all over again, during those eleven days my son was in the hospital.

How I Spent My Summer Vacation

Another element of the *someone to love* part of the happiness equation is how it feels to give of yourself to someone so completely that he or she fills many of your waking hours. Whether you're taking care of an older parent or a sick child or simply raising your family, giving, doing, caring for and just being there for someone else is one excellent way to fall into the delicious "someone to love" delirium.

Oh, it may seem like tedium. Day after day, work: cooking, cleaning, washing clothes, driving them here and there, day after routine day. But believe it or not, it's when we're in that careful caring-for-and-doing-for-someone-else mode that we discover the deeper, more meaningful happiness factor. Like everything else, I had to learn this lesson for myself.

On a warm sunny day in September 1999, I said good-bye to Andrew as he walked toward the jetway to get on a plane for Tempe, Arizona, to begin his second year of college at Arizona State University. I cried a few tears, then forced myself to turn around and walk through the airport and back to my car. I drove home tearfully. *I miss him already!* I whined to myself.

At home I wandered through my empty house recalling days of what turned out to be our very last summer together. He was, after all, almost twenty years old, and I think I knew that perhaps the next summer he'd stay on campus and work to help pay his college expenses.

After wandering around my empty house that day in September, I turned on my computer. Of course, the first thing I did was send him a note that would be waiting for him when he returned to the land of cactus, coeds and college. Later that day when my e-mail inbox filled up with the typical barrage of jokes, quotes, stories and miscellaneous blather, I noticed a quote I'd never seen before. It said,

> *People will forget what you said. They will forget what you did. But people will never forget how you made them feel.*

Hmm, I thought. *People will never forget how you made them feel.* I thought about how Andrew had made me feel that summer. I wondered how I'd made him feel.

The previous May I'd cleared my schedule for most of the summer, thus avoiding the health-and-mind-destroying stress that could easily creep into my life had I been working full time. Andrew was on his way home from his first year of college to have the surgery that could eradicate the ulcerative colitis that he'd been plagued with for nearly three years. His entire colon would be removed and a temporary colostomy bag attached to his side for the next six months. Not the sort of thing a tall, handsome nineteen-year-old college student looks forward to.

The surgery was successful, but for the first six weeks after surgery he didn't want to see or talk to any of his friends. He just wanted to recuperate. So I was his only conversation partner. By Week Three I started nagging him daily to go for slow, easy walks with me in the evenings. It was what the doctor ordered, and during those humid treks around the neighborhood I heard about the plans he had for a part-time job when he returned to college. I heard about the classes he wanted to take. I heard about the motorcycle he hoped to buy when he returned to the land of high heat and low humidity, about the trips he wanted to take on that motorcycle. He shared the possibilities of what he could do with a German major and wondered out loud what life would be like in his first apartment.

Thinking he should be healing faster, I encouraged him to get out more. "Call your friends," I begged. "You should be walking more, getting more exercise. You should invite your friends over, do stuff. It's been four weeks! You should be healed by now. How will you ever be ready to head back to college next month?"

"I'm not ready, Mom. I just don't want to see anyone yet," he said in a quiet voice.

Even though professional baseball isn't my favorite pastime, I suggested that Andrew and I go to a Milwaukee Brewers game one evening in July. Baseball is one of Andrew's passions, and sure enough, he jumped at the chance.

At Milwaukee County Stadium that night, the game progressed the way most ballgames do. We watched the game, we watched the people, we ate junk food. Then suddenly, just after the seventh inning stretch around 9:30 PM there was a power failure and the enormous lights that lit up the field went out. The stadium and field were left in a hazy darkness, and within a few minutes the players retreated into the dugouts. Because the score was Brewers 10, Kansas City 3, many people got up and left for home. Others headed for the refreshment stands, blew bubbles or sang songs in groups. The favorite seemed to be the "Beer Barrel Polka."

When Andrew decided to take a walk around the stadium, I pulled a book out of my backpack and started to read under the few dusky generator-powered lights that were still on in the grandstand.

Twenty minutes later I looked up to see that the field was aglow with bright lights once again and the game was ready to resume. I couldn't believe my eyes. I hadn't even noticed when the lights came back on. Andrew said they'd come on very gradually over the entire thirty-minute period.

Gradually, huh? They went from total darkness to bright enough to play ball and I hadn't even noticed?

I started to think about Andrew's healing. He'd gone from major surgery to cheering for the Brewers in four weeks and I hadn't really noticed that he'd been getting a little better each day . . . gradually. I'd been too concerned about pushing him to exercise harder, sleep less, take fewer pain pills, do a few chores and call his friends to notice that he was walking tall, eating normally and anxious to get out to see his beloved Brewers.

I learned a good lesson that day about how to be patient and more understanding when my loved ones are healing. I learned that it's a gradual process. From that moment on I let Andrew be in charge of when he would do things around the house or with his friends. My spirits lifted and so did his. Loving him, the right way, made me happy, really, truly happy.

A few weeks later he started asking questions about cooking. He was planning to move into his first apartment when he returned to school, instead of living in the dorm as he had the year before. I filled a suitcase with dishes, silverware, pots, pans and spices and tucked in two boxes of macaroni-and-cheese for his first day's meal in his new apartment.

By the end of the summer my son was healed enough and had enough energy to act like a typical college kid again. He and his friends made it to four or five more Brewers games, complete with tailgate cooking on a grill.

When I got home from the airport the day he returned to college, I busied myself cleaning his bedroom and bathroom thoroughly. I put away all the junk a nineteen-year-old boy adds to those rooms in three month's time. I even took down the eight-by-six-foot Beastie Boys poster that had hung over his bed for three years. Since he'd decided to stay at ASU the following summer to make up the credits from the classes he had to drop because of his illness and surgery, I decided there was no reason to have to look at life-size Beastie Boys each time I walked past his room.

That night I had three brownies and two glasses of milk for supper. It was quite a change from the efforts I'd made all summer to prepare nutritious meals for my son while keeping to the special diet he had to be on while his body healed.

I thought back to our summer of extremes. I recalled the awful hours watching Andrew fight horrific pain in the hospital the week after his surgery. Then it was slow, gentle walks on the bike path in the evenings as we both shared our dreams for the future. It was the world's messiest bathroom for nine weeks, and now one so clean and sparse it seemed to have lost its personality. It was a summer about food, helping him to adjust to a new diet and teaching him how to cook at the same time. It was a summer about love—lots of love. Hugs in the morning and chocolate malts on our way home from the doctor's office.

After he left I noticed that the house was so quiet that I could hear the leaves falling outside. I thought about that quote: *"People will forget what you said. They will forget what you did. But people will never forget how you made them feel."*

I know neither Andrew nor I will remember everything we said to each other during the summer of 1999. And I know we'll both forget much of what we did together. But I doubt if we'll ever forget how we made each other feel.

I hope I made him feel safe, well cared for, and comfortable during the summer after his surgery. I do know for certain that he made me feel needed and loved. And because of that I have to say it was the best summer of my life.

See why having someone to love is the first thing we need to be happy?

Family Reunion

Another surefire way to learn about the importance of having someone to love is to have a family reunion. I organized one for my immediate family one June in what was then my home in Oak Creek, Wisconsin. When the long weekend was over and the last child delivered to the airport, the last set of sheets and towels washed, folded and put away, the last of the leftovers eaten or tossed, I had a quiet moment. It's over, I thought. It's really over. Twelve days of houseguests, with three days of family reunion stuck in the middle.

How is it, I wondered, that one man, Edward J. Kobbeman, a fighter pilot in World War II, can get married in 1944, have three children, and end up with a family that has swelled to two dozen people? All but four of them were at my house for the long Father's Day weekend family reunion that hot June. Jeanne, my oldest, arrived from New York the Thursday before Father's Day and stayed until the Tuesday after. My youngest, Andrew, arrived by plane from Arizona the Saturday of the reunion and stayed for ten days. But on the big weekend itself, the one we officially called "the family reunion," there were twenty of us: Dad (the fighter pilot), Bev (our beloved stepmother), my brother and sister, their spouses, myself, my children, three of their spouses, eight of Dad's nine grandchildren, three of his six great-grandchildren and one niece's boyfriend. Twenty people in all, staying at my house.

How does it work, these American family reunions, where people come from sea to shining lake, from north, south, east and west, from states near and far, in planes and three-family vans and descend upon one city, one home and make merry? It's simple: You come, you talk, you cook, you eat, you drink, you play, you gossip, you eat again, drink, play, look at photo albums, crack jokes, laugh like hyenas, play basketball, baseball, Frisbee, cards and take turns holding the family's newest baby. Then, without warning, your only brother, out bike riding with his wife on the second day, calls on his cell phone out of breath with excitement.

"Quick, tell everybody to get down here . . . to the railroad tracks. The country's largest still-running steam locomotive is making a historic run across America and it'll be passing through in seven minutes! You'll never see this again." You'd have thought it was Christmas morning and Joe was certain that Santa was going to deliver a new bike or his first model train with a real whistle and a trestle and everything.

"Seven minutes?" I stuttered, "How can we all get there in seven minutes?"

"Just get everybody in the cars and get on down here! It's only a mile or so."

Well, believe it or not, the entire family raced for the vans, piled in and we got there in plenty of time. One thing about my old-fashioned American family, it doesn't take a whole lot to entertain us.

The great steam engine and its dozen or so old-fashioned cars zipping across America was a little late so we waited in the hot sun by the railroad tracks, knowing full well that that mighty engine was not even going to slow down at the railroad crossing in our sleepy little suburb town, in spite of the fact that there were at least two dozen other folks gathered to see a bit of history in the making.

We all stood around looking google-eyed, staring down the railroad tracks, waiting for the monster steam engine and its passengers. We talked. We made jokes.

Dad and Joe filled us in on the details of what we were about to witness. All the kids, including my nearly-fifty-year-old brother, put pennies and quarters on the tracks so the steaming beast could pulverize them into worthless pieces of metal.

We talked some more, strained our eyes to see if we could spot the train coming, cracked a few more jokes about how this was the most excitement we'd had since the pigs got loose at the county fair and put a few more pennies down on the tracks.

Finally the big black beast roared toward us from the distance, coming closer and closer, as adults whisked the little redheaded grandchildren away from the tracks. And *whoosh*, there she was—whistles blowing, steam flowing, tracks clacking from the weight, going what seemed like warp speed and *whoosh*, ten seconds later . . . gone.

All the giggling kids, aged eighty-two on down, gathered our now-useless and paper-thin change amidst the weeds and gravel alongside the tracks, headed back to the vans and drove home. It was exciting, all right. Well, maybe not that exciting, but the thing is, we did it together as a family. From Dad, the octogenarian head of our crew, down to three-month-old Chloe, we were simply a family at a reunion waiting for a train, then eager to get home again to finish what all families do at reunions: gather, talk, eat, drink, laugh, play and sometimes drop everything to go see a train pass. The activities don't really matter. The most important part is the gathering . . . and the love. *Someone to love.* And if you're really lucky, you have lots of someones to love.

Cousins by the Dozens

Love stretches out from your immediate family like an octopus reaching for shellfish. Often you don't have to look further than first cousins. I have twenty-one cousins on my Dad's side and eight on my Mom's—twenty-nine first cousins altogether. One died in her twenties of lupus. Another died in his forties. Of the twenty-seven left, there are fourteen males and thirteen females, all born between 1937 and 1957. Eleven of them live in Illinois; the rest are in Alaska, California, Colorado, Florida, New Jersey, Ohio, Texas, Utah and Wisconsin. I love my cousins. Seven of the women and I are as close as if we were sisters. In fact, I call them my sister-cousins.

The backgrounds, diversity and strength-under-adversity among my twenty-seven first cousins are what I like most about them. Eleven of them are the children of an Illinois farmer who was accidentally electrocuted in a farm accident when the youngest was six months old and the oldest nineteen. One became a priest, ordained in Rome. One is a farmer. One left the family with her young child in 1975 and disappeared for twenty-three years, only to surface for a few weeks and then leave again.

The eight first cousins on my mother's side were the children of a colonel and a major general in the Air Force. All eight are college graduates and wealthy by anyone's standards. One has her PhD and runs various university departments. Cousin Barclay, the only boy in the family in his early forties, owned the largest cable company in the United Kingdom for awhile. But I haven't seen cousin Barclay for years. Few of us have. Money, remember, takes a lot of time.

My seven favorite sister-cousins are Judy, Kathleen, Marta, Jean, Karen, Meta and Mary Beth. Four from my Dad's side, three from my Mom's. Their careers are varied: X-ray technician, teacher, beautician, architectural estimator, two nurses and a university director. They are the most fun, diverse, interesting women you'd ever want to meet. Four of the seven are divorced, three have remarried. The eight of us have mothered twenty-two children. And, oh, the adventures we've had!

Judy, Marta and I were born within four months of each other and grew up in the same community. Judy and I went to school together for twelve years. Jean and I were college roommates for a year. Kathleen and I raised our preschoolers together in St. Louis for five years. Marta and I giggled and gabbed our way through my angst when I moved back to my hometown after my divorce. Mary Beth and I have had great conversations about life and love including one while we swam in the Atlantic Ocean together. Meta became a mothering mentor for me as I watched her raise her family from afar. Karen and I shared many cups of tea at her house and mine when I still lived in Wisconsin, as we hashed over the idiosyncrasies of our family.

Families come in all sizes and styles, with a variety of ideals, standards and goals. Some of my cousins are successful careerwise, some not so successful. Some are healthy, others sick and some have died before their time. Some are happy, others just so-so happy. The rich ones don't seem to be any happier than the ones who struggle from paycheck to paycheck. One of the happiest is Marta, the beautician, who is loved by everyone in town and has an upbeat personality and a rollicking sense of humor that makes every haircut an adventure.

My twenty-seven first cousins and I are as diverse as they come but we love each other, cherish our mutual ancestral heritage and bond together easier than sliding butter over a hot ear of corn. We respect our differences and remain close for one simple reason. We are family. We have roots in common. Ties that bind. *Someone to love.*

Traveling With My Father

Sometimes it takes intense, day-in, day-out togetherness to help you understand the depth of your love for someone. I have loved my father, who was born in 1919, since my first memories, heightened, no doubt, by photos of me as a baby snuggled in his arms on cold winter days in Illinois. Dad's been there for me through good times and bad and his sense of fun and creativity help me put him on a pedestal that he's never come close to falling from. But the thing about having someone so devoted to you that you love so much is that you take him or her for granted.

I never actually thought very hard about the depth of my love for Dad until August of 1998. That's when Dad, seventy-nine years old at the time, and my then seventy-four-year-old stepmother Bev offered to help me, a single parent, take my youngest son, Andrew, to college in Tempe, Arizona, over eighteen hundred miles from Milwaukee, Wisconsin. Dad and Bev not only offered their car, but their driving skills as well.

We four set out on a beautiful August morning in Dad's packed-to-the-rafters Ford Taurus wagon complete with the rack he'd made for Andrew's bicycle on top of the car. Twelve hours later, by the time we rolled into Kansas City, Andrew was so sick he ended up in the emergency room of a local hospital for the entire next day. The doctors told me to fly him to Arizona rather than keep his six-foot three-inch frame bent up in the car for three more days. So, at Dad's insistence, we two jetted our way to Phoenix while Dad and Bev drove across Kansas, Oklahoma, Texas, New Mexico and Arizona in the sweltering heat.

In the meantime, Andrew and I were enjoying the hotel pool and relaxing. Talk about a guilt trip!

When Dad and Bev arrived, we unpacked their car and spent the next two days getting Andrew settled into college life. The following day the temperature soared into the 106 degree range, which was a good thing or I'd have been a blathering, sobbing mess of a mother saying good-bye to her youngest child. As it was, I couldn't wait to get back into Dad's air-conditioned car and begin the planned post-campus vacation with my folks. There on the sidewalk in front of Andrew's dorm we said our good-byes and headed north.

Dad, Bev and I spent the next two weeks together visiting every national park, canyon and monument between Tempe and home. Altogether Dad, Bev and I were together twenty-four-hours-a-day for twenty-one days straight. Imagine three weeks with your folks, driving, eating and sleeping in the same room. Imagine doing that without a cross word from anyone during the whole trip. Well, okay, I'll 'fess up. Dad did get a little miffed, which means he pointed out my shortcomings when I did the following:

1. Forgot to lock the car one night at a hotel. (Lucky we had a car the next morning, he said.)
2. Left the car lights on for a couple hours at a tourist stop. (Lucky we still had a battery charge, he said.)
3. Didn't see the BUMP sign and flew over a huge one slamming the bottom of the car into the pavement. (Hard on the shocks, he said.)

Of course, I felt lower than a boll weevil abusing my father's beautiful car like that, but one thing about our family is that nobody holds a grudge for longer than two minutes. After each sin of mine Dad harrumphed for two minutes, then we both started blabbing like nothing happened.

When we arrived back at their home in Illinois and I was getting ready to head home to Wisconsin, Dad actually apologized for being impatient with me those few times. This guy swats me with a feather when I deserve to be hit with a verbal two-by-four and then *he* apologizes.

Dad kept a diary of our trip as we paraded from one perfect picture-postcard scene to another in Arizona, Utah, Wyoming and South Dakota. He related the wonders of the Grand Canyon, Utah's Canyonlands, Bryce and Zion National Parks, Dinosaur National Monument, Crazy Horse, the Badlands, Wall Drug, the Corn Palace in South Dakota and finally the great

Mississippi River. His last entry on the final day after we had arrived safely at their home, says, "After we unloaded the car, Bev checked the messages on the answering machine and got the surprise of her life. She had won first prize at our parish ice cream social raffle. What a country!"

What a country, indeed. From the Great Lakes to the Grand Canyon we saw it all. But it wasn't the country that amazed me the most. It was my parents. When I told my friend Jean, the psychologist, about the three week trip with my father and stepmom, Jean responded, "Not many people would be able to pull off one week of harmonious car travel with their parents, let alone three. I hope you appreciate the specialness of your relationship."

Believe me, I know how special it is. I know that what we have today is special because of my dad's amazing strength of character. As I was growing up I watched him closely. He was just as good and kind and patient then as he is now. What a country! What a dad! *Someone to love* with all my heart.

The Stuff of Good Marriages

My dear friends Wally and Shirley were married in 1953. Now in their seventies they are still in love, very active, healthy and enjoying life to the fullest. Since I'm not married I am always fascinated by how good marriages actually work. How, when you find that one *someone to love* "til death do you part,'" do you make it work?

A few years ago I helped Wally and Shirley move from their condo in Florida to a new home a few blocks away. We three worked for four days straight packing, hauling and unpacking boxes. Wally made long lists every day of things he had to do at the new house. Fix the door locks, put the garage shelves together, learn how to care for the pool, fix this, change that, unpack the seventy boxes in the garage.

Shirley and I kept busy lining the shelves in the kitchen, pantry and bathrooms and then unloaded at least a hundred boxes and found places for everything. We sorted, piled, swept, decorated, arranged, rearranged and laughed our way through the move.

Tensions mounted a few times between husband and wife, as they always do during the most stressful times in our lives. Moving is right up there with death of a spouse, loss of a job, disease and divorce as a big stressor.

One thing I learned about marriage from Wally and Shirley is the importance of an equitable division of chores, especially after both parties are retired. Shirley says they had a big sit-down powwow one evening and together they made two lists of work to be done on a regular basis for each of them. Shirley typed the lists and taped them to the inside of the kitchen cabinet. Here they are, in marriage-saving detail.

SHIRLEY: Grocery shop; fix dinner; make granola, bake bread, cakes, muffins, etc.; vacuum and wash tile floors; dust all furniture; wash and iron clothes; balance checkbook and pay bills; feed cats and clean litterbox; make coffee; clean oven and refrigerator; clean and wax bathroom and kitchen sinks and countertops; trim bushes, tend flowers and garden.

WALLY: Last-minute shopping; fix lunch; vacuum carpets; fold clothes; check bills; empty dishwasher; make bed; clean toilets and shower; fill soap dispensers; maintain auto repair; sweep garage; put out garbage, daily papers and recycle box; pest control; repair outside stuff; wash and wax cars.

As long as both parties agree to their division of chores, it's amazing how well this system works. Sometimes when I visit, Shirley is outside trimming bushes while Wally's inside fixing lunch.

The grit, grime, gusto and glory of household chores are very much like marriage itself. To make it work, accept the fact that little snits are bound to happen. The important thing is to try to get over them in less time than it takes to slam a door. No pouting allowed. Take a deep breath and crack a joke. Works every time. Also, talk about what each of you expects from the other. Write down the things each of you will be responsible for and then do your chores without prompting from the other.

Time to go. I think Wally has lunch ready. I love it when a man cooks. But mostly I love watching Wally and Shirley who have most definitely found that even after all these years of living together as husband and wife, they are still very happy. *Someone to love* makes it so.

A Celebration of Life and Love

A few days before Valentine's Day 2002 I received an e-mail from a good friend. I was already in the annual pre-Valentine's Day funk that propels single women like me who don't get candy, flowers, Valentines and fancy dinners on February 14th to justify our disdain for the holiday. Many of us believe it's just an overly commercial fabrication created by the card companies, flower shops and candy manufacturers. Single people who aren't in a relationship desperately try to ignore all the hype while going about our daily business during the weeks before the holiday.

But then that darn e-mail showed up on my screen. It was from my old friend Ray, who still considers himself a newlywed, even though he and his bride tied the knot in August of 1999. You'd think by now they'd get over the fact that they're still blissfully in love or at least try to tone it down a bit.

Two months before Ray sent me the e-mail, he'd been

hospitalized for a bad case of pneumonia that left him weak and at home for the next two months, under the watchful eye of Geri, his beloved bride, as he calls her.

Ray's letter talked about a daylong Valentine celebration he and Geri had on the day when he finally felt well again. He wrote:

> Our celebration yesterday began by thanking God for all His help ever since I had the scare exactly two months ago. After antibiotics, taking it easy, and especially all the help and support from my beautiful resident physician (who wouldn't even let me take out the garbage for a couple weeks) I can say I'm nearly as good as ever. A great reason to celebrate.
>
> And celebrate they did. Ray described their day in detail:
>
> It began with breakfast at "1 Potato 2," exciting, huh? Then four walking trips around the local mall. Not much to you, maybe, but very significant for me, since just one round trip wore me out at first. After that we just had to stop at a favorite local coffee shop where we met friends, then went to see the movie, A Beautiful Mind. We capped off our excursion at one of Milwaukee's famous Friday fish fries before going home for an exciting card game.

A few days later I heard from Ray again. His "celebration of life" continued.

> And the beat goes on! This evening we're taking in a St. Valentine "Candlelight Evening for Couples" at our church, including liturgy, presentation, sharing and prayer, followed by a delicious romantic candlelight dinner. The special program gives couples insight into their own interactions and helps them

> strengthen their relationship.
>
> We have so much to celebrate and be thankful to God for, especially for His bringing Geri and me together. Heck, I'm so darn happy that God brought us together that I want to shout it from the house tops! We're sure you have lots to be thankful for too. So, go ahead and celebrate. And be thankful every day of your life. And maybe just once in a while, enjoy a whole day of celebration. You don't need to find a reason. We all have many reasons to celebrate if you just think about it.

Ray's letter changed my whole attitude about holidays and celebrations. I will never again get wistful or jealous of my happily married friends during Valentine season. Valentine's Day may not visit me with a rainfall of heart-shaped baubles, fancy cards or romantic dinners. But I sure can create a Valentine's Day that is a celebration of its own.

After reading Ray's letter on Valentine's Day 2002, I went out and bought my favorite treat, a box of crunchy milk-chocolate Dove ice cream bars and then enjoyed every single bite of one when I got home. Later, I called up my kids who lived out of town and state and we all chatted like jaybirds. Then I prepared half a dozen cheery cards to send to my cousin's husband who had terminal cancer. Then I finished a craft project to give to my oldest granddaughter for her birthday. I learned that the feeling of celebration is more about knowing you have *someone to love* and that *doing for others* is a big part of that love. All in all, it was a fabulous Valentine's Day, heartfelt to the core because I busied myself actively loving other people. *Someone to love.*

Another thing I learned from Geri and Ray is the fact that we certainly don't need a national holiday to plan a celebration. Pick a day, any day, and when you get out of bed in the morning, declare it a grand day of celebration. Watch your happiness factor soar. We can celebrate freedom, family, good health, career, home, church, neighbors, friends . . . everybody and everything. Most of all, we can celebrate all the people we love. *Someone to love.* Actively, purposely loving someone else is what makes us happy.

On my next day of celebration I may not pack as many things as Ray and Geri did into their day of celebration (who's got that much energy?) but it'll be grand just the same. Oh, did I mention that when Ray wrote that letter to me he was seventy-eight years old and his bride just eight years his junior? Hard to keep up with those two. I can tell you this: Having known Ray for many years before he met Geri, his act of finding *someone to love* changed his life so much it still makes my head spin.

How Different Can Sisters Be?

I have one blood sister, Catherine, one sister-in-law, Linda, a best friend, Melanie, seven sister-cousins and a number of other wonderful women friends. And then there's Brenda.

When I sold my big house in Milwaukee and moved into a small condo thirteen hundred miles away in Florida, I met Brenda at the big swimming pool across the street. She lives in the seven-story building a few hundred feet from my own two-story building. The day I met her I knew there were lots of differences.

Brenda is a born-and-raised New Yorker, living in Florida just seven or eight months a year. After living in five different states, I moved to Florida to be a permanent resident.

Brenda's married, I'm not. She's Jewish. I'm Catholic. Brenda has one son and no grandchildren. I have two girls, two boys and eight grandkids, scattered in Ohio, Wisconsin and California.

I can bike twenty miles without blinking. Brenda complains going turtle speed on a bike after two miles. A retired home-economics and art teacher, she's much more creative than I. Brenda is a self-admitted hypochondriac. I have to be on my deathbed before I even think of going to the doctor.

Brenda's shorter than I with a roundish figure and one-half-inch-long black hair forming a cute cap on her perfectly-shaped head. I'm taller with bigger bones, large calves and gray-blonde hair going every which way. We definitely do not look like sisters.

I'm not a telephone person. Brenda can yak on the phone for half a day every day. She's learning to keep our calls short. I'm learning to call her once in a while.

In spite of our differences, Brenda and I have become sisters of the heart. What binds us together? Quite possibly our differences, but also faith and laughter. She's teaching me Yiddish. I've learned to kvell, kvetch and kibbitz with gusto. Brenda taught me how to make matzoh ball soup and matzoh brei (eggs and crushed matzoh fried up like French toast . . . yummy!). Our lunches out are often at a Jewish deli.

I dragged her to our Christmas concert at church. She was expecting *Jingle Bells* and *O Christmas Tree* but instead discovered the birth of Jesus and the beauty of Christian music. Our Judeo-Christian backgrounds are wearing off on each other as we learn about each other's customs and beliefs.

I confide in Brenda about my relationships. She and Paul have been happily married since 1969. Since 1968 I've been married, divorced and annulled twice and I've got a million questions for her about how to make a relationship work.

It seems that Brenda and I are always on a diet. For a year before her only child was married she was on the wedding diet. I've gained and lost enough weight in my lifetime to float the

Queen Mary. But oh, it's so much fun to talk to her about feeling fat, exercising more, eating less, whining, celebrating and cajoling each other into different size clothes.

Once when Brenda accused me of having gunboat feet (I do, size ten), I shot back that she had a big butt. Those words became the darts we throw at each other in jest when we need verbal weapons for a sisterly dig.

But most importantly Brenda and I laugh a lot. We paint ceramics together and laugh our heads off for hours while we create the most amazing ceramic patterns and then always go for ice cream at the little log cabin ice-cream parlor next door.

We giggle about dumb stuff. We bicker when planning a party about little details, then laugh about how well everything turned out.

Brenda bought me a goofy-looking long, lime-green fat chenille-type scarf for my birthday. I wrapped it around my head, stuck in my Billy Bob buck teeth, took a photo of myself and sent it to her in a clear envelope for the world to see.

Sometimes we just laugh out loud with joy over the splendor of our lives. We wonder, *how is it that we are so fortunate to not only be living in paradise but to have found such a friend.* A sister friend. Someone to love.

Excuse me, it's time to call Brenda and see about a bike ride. A slow one.

Chapter Three

Something to Do

The quality of a person's life is in direct proportion to their commitment to excellence, regardless of their field of endeavor.

—Vince Lombardi

If we want to be happy, we have to have something worthwhile to fill up our days. We need to be productive members of society, working to make things better in our world. Whether we have a job outside the home or we work at home taking care of our families, most of us have plenty to do, so it isn't a problem. Many older retired people actually don't have enough to do and that's when they need to get off the sofa and volunteer their time to help others if they want this piece of the happiness puzzle.

Even when we plan a vacation where we can escape to an island and do nothing for days on end, we invariably get tired and bored with nothing to do. After a few days of sun, sand, sea and surf, we sit up, dust off the sand and say, "Hey, let's do something today! Let's go exploring. Let's go into town. Go for a hike. Try snorkeling. Visit the local museum. I can't stand sitting here another minute!"

The trick is finding the right things to do. Noble things,

interesting things, helpful things.

Creativity Helps

My friend Brenda spends half the year in East Rockaway, a suburb of New York. Brenda is one of the most creative people I know. She ought to be. She was born with loads of creative talent and was a home-economics teacher during her three-decades-long career. During the first two years of our friendship she painted ceramic teapots, made quilts, painted tiny two-inch-square paintings, designed and crafted wild and wonderful purses, and quilted eight-foot-square *chuppas* for two Jewish weddings. But during one summer when she and her husband lived on their boat, she didn't have any creative supplies with her. It wasn't her happiest time.

The following year, before Brenda and her husband left again for New York, she sent me an e-mail.

> *I started making my green bag and it's looking fine, very funky. I just love it. Then I'm starting a baby blanket for Eden Jane Rose, my newest great-niece. I bought great fabric for it. I have now realized that last summer's deep blue funk was because I wasn't creating anything. I really need that creative process to be happy. This season, here, I had none of that blue funk because every day I woke up thinking about what part of my project I was working on, and how to best do that job. A delicious process.*

Brenda has figured it out. She understands that in order to be happy we all need *something to do.* And for most of us, something to do includes creating something from scratch. Whether you like to build cars from scratch, plant flower gardens, quilt, paint, design buildings, make greeting cards, invent new products, bake exquisite pastries, build swing sets, can pickles, crochet scarves, teach, preach or reach for the moon, or any number of other endeavors, the very act of creating is a huge boon to our ability to be happy. We just have to have that delicious sense of *something to do.*

Right Livelihood

I once heard a story about three bricklayers who were hard at work. Someone stopped by and asked, "What are you building?"

The first bricklayer responded gruffly, "I'm laying bricks."

The second one said simply, "I'm building a wall."

The third one stood tall, wiped his brow, held out his arms to the heavens, and with great enthusiasm and obvious pride said, "I'm building a cathedral!"

I've thought about that story many times since 1992, when I quit my job at the radio station to stay home and became a self-employed writer and speaker. On the days when I feel like whining because I'm not making enough money or because medical insurance is so costly for the self employed, or because there's no one at the water cooler to talk to . . . those are the days when I think of the third bricklayer and remind myself that I am fortunate, indeed, to be doing work that I love.

For those of us who choose to work in offices at home, it isn't always easy to be passionate self-starters who plan the various projects we must do each workday. It isn't easy to produce material and send it off to whoever buys our product or ability. But on those days when I procrastinate and putter around the house instead of being productive in my office, I notice that I feel sluggish and depressed at the end of the day. But when I put in a full day at my computer or I'm out speaking to a group of people, my energy level zooms and my happiness quotient soars. That's when I know that work, good hard work, work that I love doing, is an important ingredient for happiness.

I know one thing for sure: I'm never going to retire from this job. I've seen too many people who retire commute directly into the recliner in front of the TV set. Their health fails, they gain weight and lose interest in life. Boredom sets in, big time.

That's not the life for me, whether I'm sixty, eighty or ninety-five. I've learned that it's work that puts the sizzle in my life, especially work that makes someone else's life better, like the bricklayer building a cathedral. If your work is unpaid volunteer activities, bravo for you. You're getting a positive double whammy. You're not only doing something with your life, you're making life better for others. If your work makes you feel good about life in general and about your place in the universe, then you're going to be happy.

As a writer and speaker, I know that writer's block and boredom are caused by procrastination and laziness. But if I get up every morning, hit the computer and make a list of things I need to do, I can pretty much guarantee a good productive day.

Ask anyone who is self-employed. It isn't easy to stay motivated and productive day after day when there's no boss hounding you to get the work done. But I've learned over the years that a number of things help. For instance, when I'm exercising regularly, eating right and staying in contact with friends who inspire me, my motivation and production soars.

In my heart, I'm building a cathedral, not just laying bricks. And for me, finding *something to do*, work that I love, work that seems to be important, is the key to deep contentment and happiness.

Old-Fashioned Hospitality

When I was a kid I remember visiting my grandparents in the tiny town of Blandinsville, Illinois, population six hundred. Grandpa and Grandma Knapp lived in a small white frame house with a squeaky porch swing where Grandma and I would sit for hours talking and talking as the swing seemed to move to the rhythm of our voices.

We didn't talk about anything important. I remember conversations about why the skin on her hands was loose and mine was tight. Or about the best way to kill those pesky weeds that grew in the sidewalk cracks. Or about the fact that Doc Borum was on vacation. Stuff like that.

At least five or six days a week, one or two visitors would stop by. These weren't planned visits, mind you. Grandma didn't phone ahead and invite Mrs. Brewster over for coffee or call to see when the Soule family could come for lunch. No, folks in Blandinsville just stopped in unannounced to do one thing—visit.

In the winter they'd visit in front of the coal stove that popped and hissed in the middle of the living room as Grandpa and Grandma and I sat in the old worn wooden rocking chairs and the guests sat on the sofa or overstuffed chair. In the summer neighbors walked over to sit a spell in the porch swing. Grandma would bring out the pitcher of lemonade made from real lemons and then pull out an extra chair or two from the dining room onto the porch so everybody could sit down. Sometimes she brought out the cookie jar and passed it around.

Every day they came. Old farmer friends who'd retired like Grandpa and moved into town. Shopkeepers on their way home from work. The preacher from the local Christian church. The town librarian.

Every summer when I spent a week or two visiting my grandparents I was amazed at the number of visitors they had. Why, they had more company in one week than my folks had in two or three months. Relaxed, friendly chit-chatty visits from friends were as much a part of my grandparents' daily lives as breathing and eating.

Today, fifty years later, I wonder what happened to that custom of drop-in-anytime hospitality. Why is it that we think we need a week to prepare for guests and that we must have every nook and cranny in our homes white-glove-inspection clean and that we must feed our visitors elaborate meals every time they come to our homes? Why can't we be more open to surprise visits from friends, relatives or mere acquaintances? What's wrong with spontaneity? If we could get back in the habit of visiting each other without a formal invitation, wouldn't our lives be easier, happier, more fulfilled?

I, for one, love surprise guests because it means I'm not *expected* to have the house clean or food prepared. I can boil water for tea, pour lemonade made from a can and pass out graham crackers if that's all I have on hand. No stress, no fuss, just my guests and me visiting without any expectations of what's to come.

Hebrews 13:2 puts it in perspective. *Don't forget to be kind to* strangers, for some who have done this have entertained angels without *realizing it!* If we're supposed to welcome strangers, imagine how we're supposed to greet *friends*! Another verse, Titus 1:8, commands us to be welcoming. *They must enjoy having guests in their homes and must love all that is good.* (TLB)

I, for one, think that's part of a problem with our churches these days. A few years ago I joined a new parish. Fourteen months later when our pastor was having lunch with my son and me, I asked, "Father, do you consider me a friendly, outgoing person?"

He laughed, "Of course."

"Well, after fourteen months of attending your parish every week, you and your secretary are the only people whose names I know."

A few months later, when that pastor moved on to a new parish, I switched to a parish closer to my home. Two weeks after my switch, the pastor there, Father Bob, not only gave a sermon about hospitality but announced that we'd be having coffee and doughnuts right in the back of the church. Not in the school gym or the parish basement, but right there in God's house where we were already gathered. I saw some old friends and met a few new ones. This one introduced me to that one. People chatted, laughed and did some of that good old-fashioned visiting.

Perhaps every congregation should create a hospitality center in the back of their church with a few wooden rocking chairs, an overstuffed sofa or two and maybe a cookie jar. We are, after all, the family of God. Shouldn't we at least know each others' names and get together for a visit once a week? The gift of hospitality is something to do that most definitely opens the door to unbridled happiness.

The other day my new neighbor Marian stopped in for a surprise visit. I quickly put on the teapot and showed her the collection of seventy different flavors of tea on my kitchen counter. She dashed home (only thirty steps, just two condos away) and returned with a bag of homemade cookies she'd just taken out of the oven. We talked and talked for over an hour, getting to know each other.

I opened up to her and talked about my relationship with my friend Jack who lives just fifty-seven steps away from my condo. She smiled, listened, asked questions and shared a bit of her own personal life. I felt happy. Why? Because this older, wiser new friend was weaving herself into the very fabric of my life, forming a quilt of many colors and designs.

I learned that day that a simple cup of tea with a new friend is a surefire way to build happiness. I like knowing Marian is just thirty steps away.

The Boomerang Effect

A few years ago I learned firsthand how *doing* for others, simply giving a few minutes of our time for someone else, can yield hours, days, months, even years, of contentment and happiness in return. My friend Barbara who lived in Cheyenne, Wyoming, wanted desperately to be a published author. Periodically, for at least twenty years, she submitted essays and articles to magazines and newspapers, but never had anything accepted.

One time Barbara sent me a copy of one of her reworked and rewritten manuscripts that I'd helped her with previously. I saw how hard she'd worked on it and liked her final version. Knowing that Barbara's eyesight was failing because of severe diabetes, I sent her piece to the editor of a newspaper. I didn't tell Barbara because I didn't want her to be disappointed again if the editor rejected it.

A month later I got a phone call from Barbara. Her voice was cracking. She sounded tearful.

"Barbara, what's wrong?"

"A friend of mine came over to read me my mail this afternoon. The last thing he came to was a big manila envelope.

A newspaper was inside with a check and a note attached saying that the editor loved my story and was publishing it.

"Pat, my story is in that very newspaper on the front page! I'm a published author! Imagine! Me, published!" Barbara paused, "I know you sent it in. How can I thank you? I was so depressed with my eye problems and then this happened. I'm so happy! I was going to quit writing. Now I'm going to tape-record my stories and find someone to type them."

I started crying as Barbara's joy raced through the phone lines and jumped right into my heart. It had taken so little of my time to put her manuscript in the mail to the editor with a quick note asking that if she decided to publish the piece to please send the check and a copy of the paper to Barbara. A twenty-minute gift of my time brought a lifetime of excitement to a woman who needed a boost in the worst way.

My gift to Barbara was like a boomerang. Her excitement at being published boosted me to submit more articles to editors myself. Barbara, who was well into her eighties when she became a first-time published author, died the following year. Since then, every time I receive an acceptance letter from an editor, I think of Barbara and thank her for teaching me to use my time wisely. *Something to do.* It's a beautiful, happy thing, especially when it comes to doing for others.

The Hammock

We were attending a big party at a beautiful home on Wisconsin's Lake Geneva when I saw it swaying slightly in the breeze . . . an inviting, big-enough-for-two hammock. I slipped in gently, relaxed a moment, then hurried back to the party.

Hurried. My whole life seemed hurried. Every minute of every day seemed preprogrammed. My whole body felt tense, yet I still hurried to work, then rushed home to take the children to baseball games, play practice and music lessons, then home to throw clothes into the washer. I hurried with my teenagers to the orthodontist, the dentist, then shopping so I could hurry home to fix supper. After dinner I'd even hurry through a storybook with my four-year-old so I could get down to my room to finish writing an article an editor wanted.

The speed with which life was engulfing me was giving me headaches. It seemed that every minute of every day was programmed. My back ached, my whole body felt tense, yet I still hurried to work, hurried home, raced to my evening class and flopped into bed at night, too exhausted to even think.

That hammock started haunting me. Wouldn't it be nice . . . ? I started to dream big dreams, but then I'd wonder if I could find time to relax in it if I bought one. Then one day, while waiting for my teens at the orthodontist, I saw an ad for a hammock just like the one we'd seen at the lake. On a healthy impulse, I ordered one.

When it arrived, my son Michael, age twelve, and I drilled holes in two backyard trees and mounted the screws and hooks that would support this new luxury. We did a fine job and the hammock looked marvelous and inviting.

Michael and I rewarded our efforts with an inaugural rest. Both of us plopped into the double-wide macramé rope hammock and chatted about what a great job we did. And we talked about other projects we might tackle together. A canvas swing in that tree over there? A small fence around the garden? We talked about school and then recaptured the excitement of the home run he'd hit the day before.

Then Andrew, age four, came bounding out of the house with unbridled enthusiasm for his first ride. Michael gave up his spot and Andrew climbed aboard.

The two of us stared at the leaves above us. "Mommy," Andrew giggled, "look at that squirrel!" We watched it scurry from limb to limb.

Then silence for a few minutes. I closed my eyes. A breeze was rocking me toward slumber. But not Andrew. "You know, Mom, I think those clouds are moving. There's one up there that looks like Dumbo. See the trunk?"

"*Uhhh, hummm*," I answered almost unconsciously.

Andrew continued to chatter, but his little body hardly moved from the curves of my own as we snuggled in the hammock.

An hour later, I realized that I was, for the first time all summer, relaxed. Totally, completely relaxed. My headache was gone. Not only had the hammock provided a place to rest, it was the perfect place to talk to the children one-on-one. A place to open our hearts, to grow closer, and to really listen.

That evening, Julia, age thirteen, spent an hour in the hammock reading. Next fifteen-year-old Jeanne plopped sideways in it to observe a colony of ants building a house directly underneath the hammock.

The next day when I returned from work, I walked right past the washing machine, grabbed a book I'd been trying to finish for over a year and headed for you-know-where.

It's funny how some rope, two wooden supports and a couple of good strong trees can change your life. Best prescription for pure happiness I ever took.

Keeping Up With Dad

Growing old doesn't scare me. No way. So what if my cholesterol is squeaking over the normal limit. So what if every single chocolate chip cookie I eat ends up attached to the outside of my stomach instead of *in* it. Yes, I exercise, but I'm not a six-day-a-week fanatic. To me, exercise is a nice relaxing eight-mile bike ride on an interesting trail meandering through parks, or an hour-long swim in the condo pool in between chatting with the other residents.

Great-uncle Collie lived to be one hundred and four. Great-aunt Peggy was one hundred when she died peacefully in her sleep. My grandfather, Porter Knapp, was ninety-three. And my dad? Well, it's downright disrespectful to even put his name in this paragraph. Born in 1919 he still looks and acts like a fit, robust gent in his sixties. Dad makes my physical activity look like someone taking a nap on the rug in Romper Room.

While I nurse an arthritic knee with Ibuprofen and refuse to go up a lot of steps, Dad's knees don't hurt a bit, anytime, anywhere. While I do slow bend-overs to nurse my aching back after standing around at a museum or a mall, he's jumping onto his bicycle for a trip to the bakery for his favorite pastry.

It gets better. Two months before he turned eighty-three Dad rode shotgun in a two-seat stock car driven by a professional in a Winston Cup-style qualifying run at Chicagoland Speedway. He went around the mile-and-a-half track three times going one hundred sixty miles per hour. I like to think I've inherited some of his adventure genes but my speed is more like doing twenty-five miles an hour on my bicycle going downhill.

One month before Dad turned eighty-three he rode shotgun again. Only this time it was in the right seat of a four-place Piper Cherokee airplane with my brother Joe in the left seat. Shortly after takeoff, Dad took control of the plane and proceeded to do five takeoffs and five landings by himself. He says the landings weren't as good as he wanted, which means they weren't like butter sliding off a hot ear of corn. But my brother says they were pretty darn good. It's true, Dad had been a fighter pilot during World War II in the Pacific and then was part owner of a small Beechcraft Bonanza from 1969–1972. But it had been twenty-nine years since he was in control of an airplane and at nearly eighty-three he decided to do five takeoffs and landings.

A few months before his eighty-eighth birthday Dad loaded up his two restored 1930 American Austin cars, one red roadster, one green coupe, into his giant enclosed trailer and hauled them both to the Austin car meet in Missouri. And of course he added to his trophy collection at the meet, winning first place in one division. In the past few years he's won trophies for his antique cars in Illinois, Michigan, Tennessee, Pennsylvania, Ohio and Kansas. Nothing stops this guy.

When Dad turned seventy-five he went parasailing in New Zealand. At eighty he rode in a hot air balloon in Kentucky. In July 2000, just before his eighty-first birthday, he put the pedal to the metal at the top of a mountain in Austria and joined my brother, sister-in-law and myself as we each plopped our fannies onto a sled and sped down an eleven-hundred-foot-long alpine slide.

I've always wondered about the secret to Dad's robust energy, good health and his amazing accomplishments. For one thing he keeps busy. Pour that man a cup of coffee in the morning and before he takes the first sip he's out in the barn, in the garage, the yard or the porch puttering, fixing, cleaning, refinishing, building, restoring or remodeling. He simply can't sit still for more than a few minutes.

In his eighty-third year he built my sister and her husband shelves for their garage, twelve feet long, seven feet high and two feet deep. Then he hauled them one hundred miles in his pickup truck and installed them. He finished the front of those shelves in beautiful oak, nice enough for a family room.

I suppose there are two other reasons for Dad's good health. One is that he's been happily married to Bev since 1982.

Mother died in 1979, and Bev, bless her heart, just keeps adding zest and laughter to Dad's life. The other reason is his daily nap. Every day at 2:00 PM Dad and Bev stop what they're doing and take a nap for forty-five minutes to an hour. At 3:00 PM they're up and at 'em for eight more hours of adventures and projects.

All I can say is that if I have one half of Dad's good health, energy, smarts, good hearing, chutzpah and flair for adventure when I'm his age, I will be very, very happy. Until then, I'm just eternally grateful that good genes have such a big role in our health and life span.

One thing's for sure. Keeping busy and having plenty to do every day of his life makes my dad happy. Very, very happy.

Time for my nap. See, I'm already following in Dad's footsteps.

Never Say No to an Opportunity

We all know people who never seem to have any grand adventures because they can't bring themselves to break their routine. They always come up with excuses when you suggest something different or exciting to do. Years ago, to avoid that safe, comfortable road myself, I adopted a philosophy of life that says, *Never say no to an opportunity unless it's illegal or immoral.* I decided to believe it and follow it religiously. That one sentence has handed me more than my share of adventures.

One grand adventure began in 1996 when I received a letter from a woman named Winnie Chai in Kuala Lumpur, Malaysia. She'd read a story I'd written in one of the *Chicken Soup for the Soul* books that touched her and for the first time in her life, wrote a letter to an author. Winnie's long letter was delightful. Her parents had migrated from China to Malaysia in the late 1940s. They were devout Catholics, and Winnie was educated by nuns in Malaysia and taught to speak perfect English. Winnie had never been married but longed to have a family of her own.

I was so taken by her letter that I wrote her one of the longest letters I've ever written. I told her all about my four children, my single-parent stresses and my life in America. After that we started regularly e-mailing one another.

A year later I got a phone call. "Pat, I'm in New York! First time I've ever been to the United States and I just wanted to hear your voice." Winnie worked for Panasonic in Malaysia and was visiting colleagues who worked for the company in the States. I convinced her that she needed to see another part of America and invited her to fly to Milwaukee and spend a few days with me.

Winnie arrived the next morning. We spent four days seeing the sights and getting to know each other. We e-mailed off and on for the next two years until the summer of 1999 when I received a note that said, "Pat, Chris has asked me to marry him! The wedding is September 25 and you must come! I'll even help pay your way. Please try to make it!"

Because of that philosophy about never saying no to an opportunity and knowing I could fly stand-by for pennies on the dollar because my sister-in-law worked for a major airline, I said, "Of course! Yes! I'll come."

At the time I didn't have a clue as to what the trip involved, but I soon found out. The morning of Sunday, September 19, I took the 7:30 airport bus from Milwaukee to Chicago's O'Hare Airport, waited two hours, flew twelve hours to Japan, waited there for three hours, boarded another plane for a six-hour flight to Singapore, was met there at midnight (which was really

9:00 AM the next day, my time) by a friend of Winnie's named Sreela and Sreela's uncle. They took me to the uncle's house to spend the night. The next morning he put the two of us on the bus to Kuala Lumpur, another six-hour adventure, and finally at 3:00 PM Tuesday we arrived in Kuala Lumpur, spent time at Sreela's house and at 6:00 PM Tuesday finally met up with Winnie at the church in time for choir rehearsal for the wedding.

Because the bride was busy with last-minute preparations I spent the next three days either sightseeing on guided tours or seeing the sights with a variety of Winnie's amazingly wonderful friends. On my own I visited museums, the King's palace, an art festival, a park with a sculpture garden, a batik factory and a pewter factory. Sreela, who is Indian, took me to Little India for the most marvelous tea in the world at her favorite coffee house.

Nilo, another of Winnie's friends who shared the small floor of Winnie's living room, toured Chinatown and the Central Market with me, and we attended the four separate events of the wedding day together. Nilo, an Indian Muslim raised in Malaysia, is married to an Englishman and had been living in London since the mid-1980s.

In ten days I traveled over twenty thousand miles by air, bus and car. I met dozens upon dozens of incredibly open, friendly people; ate either Malaysian, Chinese or Indian food at every meal; climbed 364 steps in the rain to see the inside of the Temple Cave (and 364 steps down!); and used bathrooms that were more primitive than outhouses, as well as elegant bathrooms that put our western ones to shame. I visited my new Malaysian and Singaporean friends in four different homes and saw four different lifestyles up close and personal. I had long, late-evening talks about what's important in life with my new friends and with Winnie and Chris. And I was part of the most amazing wedding I've ever experienced.

That week I met people from India, China, Japan and London who'd come in for the big wedding. Winnie's mother, who doesn't speak English, and I communicated with hand motions, pidgin English and lots of smiles. She told Winnie it was like a duck talking to a goose, but somehow we managed to communicate.

After the morning wedding we were treated to an Asian lunch and then witnessed the formal, traditional Japanese tea ceremony. That evening hundreds of guests at the reception were treated to an eight-course Chinese dinner at a five-star hotel. After dinner I joined the dancing in the two long lines of folks so diverse in their ethnic backgrounds that it looked like a gathering of the United Nations.

Is there an opportunity staring at you today? Say *Yes!* You'll never know where that opportunity might take you or how it might change your life. Remember, *something to do* is one of the most important ingredients to happiness. And if your *something to do* involves a great adventure, how wonderful is that?

How to Succeed in Business

In 1992, after having written over forty thousand radio commercials for various radio stations, I quit my job, my something to do. Although I liked my job and coworkers and the fun of working at a major radio and TV station, I figured there were more noble things to do with my life than try to convince people to buy things they probably didn't need or couldn't afford.

I also got tired of having nearly every business owner supply me with the same *key* elements, i.e., *quality*, *selection and service.* But when I visited those stores, I hardly ever noticed anything memorable about their service or their quality, selection or even their sales, for that matter.

Not long after I quit my job to stay home and carve out my own career in the writing/speaking world, I walked into a small convenience store. The owner had signs all over the place: No Unaccompanied Children Allowed. No Change Given without Purchase. Rest Rooms Are for Paying Customers Only. Funny thing about that store, you never had to wait in line for service because there were never that many customers around.

Just down the block was a newsstand. That business owner also had signs plastered all over the front of his small store. Change Gladly Given, No Purchase Necessary. Rest Rooms Located in the Rear. Ask about Our Comic Book Library for Children to Read While You Shop.

When asked why he was so accommodating, the newsstand owner simply said that he liked people and wanted to make their visit as pleasant as possible. No wonder there was always a crowd milling around his tiny store.

When I quit the job of writing radio commercials and became simply another consumer, I noticed a number of stores in my own neighborhood whose owners had the same attitude as the man who ran the newsstand.

For years I stopped in at one optical company to get my youngest son's eyeglasses tightened or refitted. Once when I dashed in with his glasses in two pieces because of a missing screw, I admitted to the young woman at the desk that I didn't buy the glasses there. Each time I'd offer to pay for the minor repair service I'd hear things like, "It's just a tiny screw you needed. No charge, ma'am. We're happy to do it." Or, "The nose piece was a just a little loose. No charge. Goodness, those glasses are dirty. Here, let me clean them for you."

There was also a jewelry store in my neighborhood with the same generous attitude. Once I needed to have my son's favorite tie tack repaired. The repair was done immediately by one of the owners while I waited.

"Thanks," I said, "What do I owe you?"

"Oh, nothing. It was a simple repair. Thanks for stopping in."

A few weeks later I stopped in to the same store to ask if the tiny little safety loop on a watch my son had just purchased in a different state could be replaced.

"No problem. I'll do it right now."

A few minutes later when I asked what I owed for the repair and for the small leather replacement loop, the proprietor said with a big grin, "No charge. We're happy to do it."

Well, by now my conscience was getting to me, especially since I'd never purchased anything in their store.

"Oh please, let me at least pay you something for your labor, " I protested.

The woman, who was obviously a very happy soul, smiled again, "Well, if you want, you could buy one of these Little League candy bars for a dollar."

I left the store munching on delicious chocolate wondering if I hadn't somehow been magically transported back to my small hometown in the 1950s when folks did things like that for people without blinking.

Wouldn't it be nice if all business owners bent over backward to offer little services without cost? Or they consistently tried to make each shopping experience for every customer a real pleasure? Business owners who do those things certainly reap a bountiful crop of happy, satisfied, loyal customers. Those store owners must sleep very well at night knowing that *service with a smile* truly does mean something special.

We consumers can spot a money-motivated service a mile away. But it's those business owners who genuinely want to help other people without thought of making more money . . . those are the truly successful, truly happy people. They're the ones who love having *something to do* that is laced with dignity and kindness. They're the ones who go home at night to spend time with their children, take walks with their spouses and actually bend down to smell the roses. Their *something to do* is practiced and punctuated with love. By running their businesses that way, they've allowed their careers to be the very things that help make them happy.

Funny how that works. When your *something to do* is done in a spirit of giving, with absolutely no strings attached, it's the simplest, quickest road to surefire happiness—and success.

The Amazing Technicolor Dream Table

Often *SOMETHING TO DO* has nothing to do with work, career, job or whatever it is we do to support ourselves. Sometimes it has more to do with how we spend our leisure time.

One year, knowing that none of my four children could be home with me for Mother's Day, I was in a giant funk. It wasn't that the kids were ignoring me. Jeanne had called the week before to let me know that her teaching job prevented her from flying home to Wisconsin from New York but that she was planning a four-day visit over Father's Day weekend. That was fine with me, especially since my all-time-favorite greeting card came from her years earlier on Father's Day when she was a teenager. That card proclaimed that I was "both mother and father to her." I liked the fact that she wanted to continue the tradition.

Julia and Michael and their spouses and my grandchildren, who all lived eighty and one hundred miles away in Madison and Lodi, Wisconsin, were planning to celebrate Mother's Day with me on the Thursday after Mother's Day when I had to drive to Madison anyway to give a speech. Besides, I knew that my daughter Julia and daughter-in-law Amy would be busy celebrating their own Mother's Days so I didn't feel guilty about not wanting to make the trip twice in one week.

And Andrew, my youngest, who was still in college in Tempe, Arizona, had just finished his finals and was busy working at a new job on campus. He'd decided to stay at ASU for summer school and had talked me into coming out to visit him for a week at the end of May.

So there I was, alone and lonely, when I awoke on Mother's Day. After giving in to a few weepy moments before I got out of bed, I told myself that if I kept busy all day I wouldn't have time to continue my pity party.

I got up, fixed my favorite tea, French Vanilla, and enjoyed a huge mug of it out on the deck. Then I toasted a big slice of my special homemade cinnamon-raisin-nut bread slathered with butter and cinnamon and sugar and set the plate on my recently sanded octagon-shaped wooden picnic table.

The day before I'd taken a steel brush and scratched off all the chipped varnish on the table and then used my electric sander to sand the top smoother than a granite headstone. Finally, I painted the top with white acrylic primer. As I drank my tea I decided to paint the second coat brown to match the deck floor when I got home from church.

Church that morning was not a very spiritual event for me as I sat there with all those grandmothers, mothers and children. Some were carrying beautiful long-stemmed red roses they'd purchased in the church vestibule for their mothers. Youngsters who understood the significance of this day were clamoring to be the one to sit next to their honored mom. I was almost embarrassed to be sitting there alone and glad that I'd picked a seat way in the back.

When Father Bob asked all the mothers to stand for a special blessing my eyes filled with tears. Then I caught myself. *No! I will not give in to this self-pity stuff. I will not! I will simply do something to brighten my life and get out of this depressing mood!* Suddenly I was a woman on a mission.

I looked up at the stained-glass windows and marveled at the many colors that were so pleasing to the eye. Bright colors: red, yellow, turquoise, orange and many shades of green and blue.

That's it! I thought excitedly, *I'll paint the picnic table all different colors! Multi-colored stripes.* I couldn't wait for the last song to finish.

At home I changed into my paint clothes and grabbed the box of acrylic paints. I counted the wood slats in the picnic table: nineteen, plus the eight strips forming the octagon around the perimeter which I decided to do in one color. I chose twenty small bottles of brightly colored paint. Everything from red, blue, yellow and green to pinks, lavender, aqua, orange, purple, sage, berry and sand. I lined them all up and decided which colors would look good next to which colors and then numbered the bottles from one to twenty.

I started with purple and a small paintbrush, being careful not to touch the slat next to the one I was painting. I'd paint awhile, stop to answer the phone when one of my kids called to wish me a happy Mother's Day, then head back to the deck.

It was a painstaking job. When the muscles tensed up in my shoulders and upper back, I decided to mow the grass. I'd put off that chore for days and now it was either mow or hire a goat to eat through what was starting to look like a pasture.

While I mowed I thought about the table and tried to imagine how it would look when finished. I mowed for an hour, came in for a bottle of water and headed right back to the deck. As I painted I started looking at those colors. And like most fifty-something women who live alone, I started talking to myself out loud.

"Hey, this purple is the exact same color as that suit I bought for Jeanne when she lived in California!" I'd taken a gamble when I bought the nubby purple sleeveless dress with the short-waisted jacket and sent it to my daughter, knowing her taste in clothes was quite different from mine. But Jeanne loved it and wore it often. In fact, the last time I'd been in New York she was still wearing the purple jacket with a pair of dress slacks, some eight to ten years later.

When I dipped my brush into the soft chocolate brown, I suddenly thought of the brown walnut vanity I'd purchased for ten dollars at an estate sale when I was first married in Denver in 1969. I'd refinished it right in the middle of our tiny apartment living room. When my second daughter, Julia, was in sixth grade, I'd moved the vanity with the huge round mirror into her room as a special surprise. She loved it, took very good care of it, even took it with her to college and then passed it on to her daughter Hailey.

The next color was bright Wisconsin Badger red. Boy, if that didn't remind me of Michael, my third child. Michael had not only graduated from the University of Wisconsin, where the school color is red, red and more red, but he also wore the red uniform of the UW marching band for five years. Since 1998 Michael had worked full time as the assistant director of the band, so he was still into red. Both Michael, his family and I were all Big Red fans, owning more than our share of red sweatshirts, jackets, T-shirts and other UW red apparel.

Next came a double-wide bright yellow center stripe, the same bright yellow that's in Arizona State's school colors where my youngest child, Andrew, was a junior. The yellow patch also reminded me of the scorching Arizona sun, and as I painted I recalled the day I said goodbye to Andrew when I took him to campus to start his freshman year.

On that beautiful sunny seventy-degree Mother's Day as I painted that picnic table with twenty different colors . . . blue, orange, magenta, lime green . . . each one provided me with spectacular Technicolor memories of each of my children.

It's true, I didn't get to go out for brunch with my children like many of my friends did. I didn't get to spend any time with any of them personally on that important day, but I made a Technicolor dream table that spoke volumes of motherhood memories each time I looked at it from my living room window. Happiness comes from finding *something to do*, something unusual. A project and a bucket of paint is a good place to start.

Keys to Success

Something to do is often about art. Loving it, enjoying it, creating it. Milwaukee art critic James Auer once defined the eight things necessary for survival as a full-time artist. They are:

1. Proper training
2. Perseverance
3. High standards
4. Good luck
5. Thick skin
6. Establishing a recognizable style and growing within it

7. Surprising viewers neither too much nor too little

8. An occasional, unanticipated break

I appreciate Auer's list because it helps me understand that *something to do* as a reason for happiness requires some work on my part. His list applies not only to all the creative arts including visual art, acting, dance, music and writing but to practically every career you can imagine. Those eight items certainly touched a note in my own struggle to make my living as a writer.

1. Proper training:

Whenever I teach a writing class I tell my students that to be a great writer you don't necessarily need to be highly educated, a genius or have a lot of natural talent. I always share with them one of my all-time favorite quotes from Calvin Coolidge: "Nothing in the world can take the place of persistence. Talent will not. Nothing is more common than unsuccessful people with talent. Genius will not. Unrewarded genius is almost a proverb. Education will not. The world is full of educated derelicts. Persistence alone is omnipotent." However, as a writer, I do think it's necessary to have a good basic education, a good grasp of grammar and most importantly, many interesting life experiences to write about. Hence, proper training *is* very important, especially if we're counting on our *something to do* to help keep us happy in life.

2. Perseverance:

This is the biggie. So many writers give up after a hundred or fifty or even ten rejections. In the early eighties I decided I wanted to write a regular column for archdiocesan newspapers around the county. I wrote ten sample columns. I got the names of the editors and addresses for one hundred Catholic newspapers. I personalized my query letter to each one, addressed one hundred large envelopes, made one hundred copies of each of those ten columns and sent off the packets.

How many newspapers hired me from that endeavor? One. I wrote a column for the *Florida Catholic* for three years for eight dollars a column. But I persevered and in the meantime started writing for magazines, wrote a few books and sent hundreds of stories to the Chicken Soup for the Soul books. Because I persevered, my stories made it through their slush pile of sometimes as many as five thousand entries per book—and have been published in over thirty-five of their books so far. Perseverance pays.

3. High standards:

I learned the hard way not to sell myself short. After spending way too many years writing radio commercials, I learned that I could quit and write the stories, articles, essays, columns and books I wanted to write about.

A dancer who doesn't get the break she thinks she deserves doesn't have to become a car hop. An artist who isn't getting the recognition he deserves doesn't have to paint chalk portraits at the circus. An actor who can't find work doesn't have to become a waiter. If you need money to live on, try hard to find a job that not only pays the bills but keeps your head held high in the profession itself. My daughter Jeanne is an artist. After getting her master's in fine art at Yale, she lived in New York City for four years. While she made art, she paid the bills by painting scenery for the graduate school at New York University and by teaching printmaking at Long Island University, both of which kept her surrounded by people who helped get her artwork noticed.

4. Good luck and the occasional, unanticipated break:

are very similar and yes, it's true, it's almost imperative that someone, somewhere see your work and be so impressed that they either want to pay you for it or at least see more of what you can do. I still think **perseverance** has more to do with success, however. It's about never giving up. *Never.*

5. Thick skin:

If you can't stand rejection, complaints from the public, letters that question your ideas, or the isolation of hunkering down for many, many hours a week to create in a quiet, often lonely, environment, then perhaps you're in the wrong field. Thick skin is the badge of courage of successful people.

6. Establishing a recognizable style and growing within it:

As a writer I know I'm not the next Stephen King. I don't write fiction or poetry or plays. My *something to do* is simply a career as a nonfiction, art-of-living writer, and it came about because of the ups and downs in my life. I felt compelled to unzip my soul, expose my own foibles and share what I learned by living life. The important thing is that I discovered my own style and I try to grow within it.

7. Surprising viewers neither too much nor too little:

The human psyche can only take so much change at one time. If the music or the play is too avant-garde or too discordant we start to fidget. If the dance is old, stiff, lacking in creativity, we become bored. If the writing is off-the-wall stream-of-consciousness we put the book down and turn on the TV. The key is taking the reader, listener, viewer or customer by the hand into a new world of experiences without making him or her pull back and run home.

Take another look at those eight things necessary for survival and see if they don't relate to your chosen field. Even if you're not in the creative arts, I think you still need all eight to succeed. Are you a teacher? Salesman? Medical professional?

Construction worker? Factory worker? Computer genius? Own your own company? If any of the eight keys to success are lacking in your life, perhaps that's what you need to work on to be truly successful. *Something to do* means doing it right. Accomplishing that is what makes us happy.

Overload

Life is full of warnings. Thunderstorm or tornado warnings flash across our TV screens to allow us time to prepare for bad weather. Road signs, *Slippery When Wet*, *Winding Road*, and *Detour Ahead*, give us the message to proceed with caution.

Our bodies give us warning signals, especially when we have too much to do. Tiredness, discomfort, weight loss, weight gain, shortness of breath, irritability and pain are signs telling us to proceed with caution, visit a doctor or change the pace.

One time a woman told me about her hectic life. Her full-time job, the social activities her husband's career demanded of her, the responsibility of her three children, caring for their home, food and clothing, her involvement in two church groups and a professional group, all spread her time so thin that she had nothing left for herself. Every minute of every day, weekends included, was preprogrammed and the family calendar looked like something prepared by the White House secretary.

Her health suffered. Tiredness, depression, lingering guilt, anxiety and constant criticism became a way of life. Finally, she realized she was on overload. She was definitely not happy.

At the urging of her friends, family and psychotherapist, the woman took a week's vacation and made a list of all the things she wanted to do in her life, not the ones she felt she had to do. She discovered that spending time alone with her husband and children was very important to her. She also liked her job even though it didn't leave much time for cleaning the house, cooking and doing laundry.

Rather than back down on her teaching career, she gave up the job of superwoman. She hired a woman to clean her house every other week, started taking her husband's shirts to the laundry, made plans for the family to eat out twice a week and shared the rest of the kitchen responsibilities with her husband and children, who discovered that figuring out new menus, grocery shopping and puttering in the kitchen together was interesting, if not downright fun, when they did it together.

Once that woman was able to let go of the traditional roles of woman/wife/mother and concentrate on those things which made use of her talents as a teacher, her warmth as a friend and a spouse, and her love of mothering all returned big time. Her life became fulfilling and her good health returned. She found time to smell the flowers at the botanical garden, enjoy sunsets and nights out with her husband alone, take leisurely walks by herself, fly kites with her younger son, play piano duets with her daughter and attend her older son's baseball games. Best of all, she was able to bask in the knowledge that she didn't have to be or do everything in order to be successful.

Is your life too hectic? Do you have too much to do? These days that's like asking someone if they breathe very often. Of course our lives are too hectic! Having *something to do* is a critical part of being happy, but having too much to do is a big spoiler. A deal breaker.

My hectic life slowed down considerably when my three older children went to college, graduated and started their own lives in distant towns. It also helped when I quit my job in 1992 to stay home and do what I love more than anything . . . spend more time with my youngest child and plunk away at the computer writing books.

If your life isn't stress-free and you have way too much to do, perhaps you need to eliminate some things and trim down the importance of others. Perhaps you need to stop feeling guilty if you hire someone else to do some of the work for you. Call a family meeting and explain the new division of property. *Property* being cleaning, cooking, laundry and yardwork chores.

My dear friend Shirley tells about the day she called such a meeting. "It was the day of my great fit," Shirley smiles. In fact, even today, over thirty years later, her husband and son still refer to it as *The Day Mom Threw Her Fit.*

"Wally and I were both teaching full time, but he and Scott (their only child) always managed to have time every weekend for hunting, fishing, exploring, canoeing, camping and hanging out in the garage, basement or backyard. You name it, they were the great outdoor pioneers. In the meantime, on weekends, especially, I was schlepping to the grocery store, running errands, cooking, cleaning, doing laundry, running the entire house. Finally I had it . . . my big fit. I blubbered out my complaints and woes with more anger than I'd ever exposed to the world, let alone to Wally and Scott, and then went on strike immediately thereafter. It didn't take my husband and son long to discover that part of their leisure time was, from that moment on, going to involve some of the cooking, cleaning and laundry chores. I look back on The Day Mom Threw Her Fit and see it as the turning point in our lives. From then on we were all much happier."

Sometimes when we have *something to do* and it has snowballed out of control, we simply have to call a halt, reorganize and start over.

I heard once that if the mother in a family is happy, then everybody's happy. If Mom is unhappy, watch out, there's a potential land mine around every corner.

If today's the day your family chore list is going to be

redistributed and your lives are going to become more satisfying, let me offer one bit of advice. When you call that family meeting, start by telling each person in the family how much you love and appreciate them. Diffuse the mood of gloom and doom with positive statements. Then get down to work and have your fit. Well, you don't really need to have a *fit*, per se. Fits are generally reserved for those families whose distribution of family-related work has really gotten out of hand. You may just need to quietly figure out positive ways you can all work together to make the whole family function like a well-oiled machine, with time for each of you to smell the brownies baking, flowers growing, fresh air blowing.

Perhaps we all need to have one great fit in our lives. Like Wally and Shirley, you'll be talking and laughing about it for generations. If it means giving you just the right amount of *something to do*, then by all means, go for it. Having *something to do* helps make us happy. Too much to do is a deal, back and commitment breaker. Don't let it happen.

On Ducks' Wings

When I was a kid my mother was in charge of the family budget. She kept cash in a dozen envelopes including one that said, *Repair and Improvement.* That envelope fascinated and somewhat irritated me. I couldn't understand why you needed to stick perfectly good money in an envelope that might not be needed all month, money I thought should be spent on things like a hula hoop or a pogo stick for me, instead of languishing there waiting for something around the house to break. *And what could possibly need improving?* I wondered. I thought everything in the house my dad built was perfect.

But in spite of my childish rationalizations, I certainly learned a great lesson from my frugal mother about planning ahead and being ready for emergencies or needs that change with the wind.

Another important life lesson I learned from my mother was *don't take your ducks to eagle school.* Oh sure, you can send your ducks to eagle boot camp, give them a little eagle hat, an eagle badge and a T-shirt that says, *Look at me. I'm an eagle.* You can give those ducks flying lessons from the top of the tallest tree on the top of the biggest mountain. You can dye their feathers and feed them steroids to grow bigger. But no matter how hard you try, those ducks will never become eagles. They're still going to be quacking on the pond, moving south for the winter, paddling like crazy underneath the water with their oversize flapping feet, doing what ducks love to do—raising their young in the nearest pond, creek or river.

When I was in grade school I wanted to be four things when I grew up: a doctor, airline pilot, trapeze artist and a writer. I seriously explored the possibilities of all four professions. I eventually learned the lesson about not sending your ducks to eagle school when I discovered that I had no natural talent or ability in math or science. I never got anything higher than a C in all the science classes I took in high school and college. It was obvious: I was never going to be a doctor.

The airline pilot dream lasted through high school when I actually took flying lessons from my dad, but soon realized that I'm not mechanically inclined. It still takes me ten minutes to remember which dipstick is the oil and which is the transmission fluid and where each one of them is located when I open the hood on my car. In addition to that, when Dad and I got to the point of "power off stalls" in that little airplane where Dad shut off the engine during flight to teach me how to get it started again by pointing the nose to the ground to build up speed . . . well, that simple exercise nearly did me in. I was too much of a chicken to be a real pilot.

Trapeze artist? Dad built me a stellar trapeze in our backyard and I even organized a few circuses for the neighborhood in which I was the star performer. But in the seventh grade when I hit five feet seven inches tall, and faced the fact that I'd inherited my grandmother's very large bones, I knew my torso would never fly from wire to wire, bar to bar on a high trapeze for Ringling Brothers. This duck was never going to be an eagle in the center ring.

My fourth career choice held more promise. In second grade when mother gave me an old Smith Corona typewriter to play with, I knew then that I wanted to write stories for the world to read. It was easy, joyful work with A's brightening my report cards in all my English and writing classes for sixteen years. In 1981, at age thirtyfive, I started writing as a career, writing about life, loving every vowel and consonant of the work involved.

When my children wanted to major in art, music, health promotion and wellness, and TV production in college instead of the higher paying careers of math, science, law, engineering or computer technology, I smiled and embraced their career choices with gusto. My ducks were smart enough to know they shouldn't go to eagle school. I was happy that by age eighteen they knew what their strengths and talents were and they wanted careers that utilized those natural abilities. Since then they've been happy teaching and creating art, teaching and playing music, teaching health and wellness, and flying to major league sports games all over the country for the TV industry.

Sometimes we need to stop what we're doing, take stock of our lives and ask ourselves, *Am I really happy doing what I'm doing?* Sometimes we need to pull out the *repair and improvement* envelope, sell the business or quit the job and go back to school to fine tune the natural talents we were born with so we can use them as the basis for our next career.

It's true, having *something to do* is most definitely one of the five major ingredients for happiness. Just make sure that your *something to do* is something you love and are naturally good at.

Whether we're ducks or pelicans or eagles, we all need to discover our natural, and sometimes forgotten, talents, fluff our feathers and do what ducks, pelicans or eagles do best. Everything you need to be happy in your career, the *something to do*, is right there, inside you, waiting for your dream to begin. Go ahead and fly!

The Day of the Manatees

Since my main philosophy of life has been to *Never Say No to an Opportunity Unless It's Illegal or Immoral,* I've found myself on the happy end of many adventures. Because of this philosophy it seems that I'm never lacking *something to do.*

One great adventure was the time I decided to step out of my comfort zone and, on my own, take my only sister kayaking. I'd been kayaking once before in my life ten years earlier. At that time I was with two other grown-ups who knew the ropes. But this time it was just me. *Something to do* took on a whole new feel. But first, a little history about the relationship between my sister and me.

When Catherine was born in May 1959, I was about to graduate from eighth grade. The very day she was born, my graduation gift from my parents arrived in the mail, a large turquoise clock radio. I was thrilled out of my mind to finally be able to listen to Dick Biondi's rock and roll show on Chicago radio station, WLS–AM, in the privacy of my bedroom.

Being a self-centered thirteen-year-old, the birth of my little sister took a back seat to my new radio and graduation plans. Also, the fact that I would have to share my bedroom with the little creature after she spent a few months in our parents' bedroom, was not something I was looking forward to. My only brother Joe, age four, had already laid claim to the third bedroom in our home.

It was bad enough that all through high school I had to share my room with Catherine, but after she graduated from the crib, I even had to share my bed with her arm flinging, squirmy little highness. She was a cutie, make no mistake, and I loved her very much, but being thirteen years my junior, we didn't have much in common except our last names.

When Catherine was four years old, I left for college. Four years later, I moved to Colorado, got married, had the first of my four children, moved to Missouri, then Illinois, Wisconsin and finally Florida.

The years passed and suddenly I was a single empty-nester, approaching sixty, semi-retired and welcoming my eighth grandchild into the world. Catherine, on the other hand, lived in Illinois, was married, worked full time as a first grade teacher and still had her two teenagers at home. Our lives had been pretty much out of sync since that day in May 1959, when my only sister's birth took second billing to my new clock radio.

But one day in 2005, all that changed. Catherine came to visit me for the first time without her husband or kids. We were shocked when we realized that week was actually the first time we two sisters had ever been together, alone, in our lives. Oh, we'd had plenty of visits back and forth over the years, but never without spouses and/or kids tagging along.

That week we took walks, went swimming, cooked together, dined out, watched movies, giggled, shared secrets and talked. Boy, did we talk! One day I asked if she'd like to go kayaking.

"I'd love to!" she practically shouted.

Catherine had never been in a kayak, never used a snorkel or mask and wasn't even that fond of swimming. Water sports, for me, were my life. I'd moved to Florida the year before to be in a warm climate so I could swim and enjoy the water on a daily basis.

The next day we drove two hours north and rented a two-person kayak on the shallow Weeki Wachee River that empties into the Gulf of Mexico a few miles upstream. A couple of hours into our glorious picture-postcard-perfect scene, we paddled within earshot of the only other boater we saw on the river that day, an older gentleman who seemed to know a lot about the river and its surroundings. He was canoeing with his daughter and granddaughter. We could hear him talking about the foliage, the fish and the history of the river.

A half hour later the older gentleman waved to us from up ahead, "Hey! Up here!" he whispered as loud as he could. "There's a big manatee! If you hurry and don't make any noise you can get up close."

Just then the man's daughter and granddaughter jumped into the three-to-five-foot-deep river. The mother put on a mask and snorkel and dove under the water to find the manatee. I jumped out of our kayak, swam over to the woman who surfaced with a delighted grin. She pulled off her mask, "Here, you can use this. The manatee is huge. It's right over there." She pointed to an area where the river was a foot deeper and loaded with seaweed and tree roots. I swam over quickly, did a surface dive and there in front of me was the largest underwater creature I'd ever seen. That gentle giant must have been at least eight or nine feet long and five feet in diameter. I swam slowly over to the top of him and started petting his tough, thick skin, noticing healed gouges that were probably the result of a run-in with a power-boat motor.

The minute I surfaced, I gasped, "Catherine, you have to come over here and see this!" My sister tied up the kayak and swam over to where I was.

"Here, put this on," I said as I handed her the mask and snorkel. "The manatee is right over there. It's amazing! You won't believe how big and slow and beautiful it is!"

Catherine was so excited she could hardly talk. She tried desperately to make the mask fit her small face, then slid the snorkel into her mouth as I gave her breathing instructions. The water was over her head, the slimy mangrove tree roots below were freaking her out, and her swimming skills were not as strong as mine. She panicked. "I can't do this! The mask fills up with water. I can't breath in that thing!"

I wasn't about to let my only sister miss out on an opportunity of a lifetime. "Then get on my back! I'll take you over to the manatee and you can just surface dive and open your eyes under water to see it."

My sister, who is shorter, smaller-boned and weighs considerably less than I do, jumped on my back, held on for dear life and we made our way over to the manatee. She put her head under the water, then came up quickly. "I see it! I see it!" She went back down to pet the noble creature.

Treading water like crazy, I held her arm each time she went under. She surfaced sputtering, "Oh my gosh, it's amazing! I can't wait to tell my students about this!"

At that moment the manatee began to move forward slowly. We followed it for a couple dozen yards, then it dove deeper and we lost sight of our favorite sea creature of all time.

Later, back in the kayak, as we leisurely paddled around the widened part of the river, Catherine let out a squeal. "Oh my gosh, there's another one, right alongside our boat! It's a baby manatee, look, on the left side!"

I turned just in time to see the much smaller creature, perhaps four or five feet long, dip under our kayak and rise up on the other side. The youngster ambled back and forth, criss-crossing underneath us for ten minutes, then took off in the direction of the Gulf.

Catherine and I were too stunned to speak. It was one of those God-moments where you just had to take it all in. Finally, after a long pause, she said, "Pat, this has been the best day of my life."

I caught my breath. I remembered how smart and strong I felt when I held my sister on my back so she'd feel safe enough to dive down to see the large manatee up close. Then I thought back to the day she was born. And somehow *that* day seemed to be the best day of *my* life. It was the day I became her sister. And that day on the Weeki Wachee river forty-six years later, was the day when *something to do* mingled with *someone to love* and the happiness quotient was square-rooted into perfection.

Chapter Four

Something to Hope For

You cannot put a great hope into a small soul.

—*J. L. Jones*

The one thing that prevents us from becoming a nation of babbling psychotic, depressed, stressed-out individuals during this highly stressed twenty-first century, is the third thing on my list of five ingredients for happiness: *something to hope for*. This one is imperative because without the hope that some things in our lives will change or be different or get better, we just have no reason to look to the future. Quite simply, having a hope or a dream makes us happy.

Why do you think so many older people in nursing homes are so unhappy? They have no one to love, little to do and nothing to hope for. Many just sit around in wheelchairs waiting to die. Hope is such a splendid gift because it buoys us up in times of tragedy, bad health, lost jobs, death of a loved one, divorce or any of life's pitfalls.

Let's start with an assignment. Please take an index card and write down your dream. Write down at least one thing you'd like to do, accomplish or experience before you die. Something that will make you happy once you do it. Place that card on your refrigerator, on top of your computer or on the bathroom mirror, some place where you'll see it every day. And then get busy making that dream come true.

Make sure your dream is something you can control. Winning the lottery doesn't count. Making our dreams come true is our responsibility, not someone else's doing or just good luck.

In 1999, I asked women at my SWILL group to share their dreams or goals. Connie said she wanted to become an accomplished writer and make enough money to also be a philanthropist. Her first dream may take twenty years, as it does most writers, and the second may be out of her control. Ideally, she'll fine-tune her goal into something like selling one article to a magazine in the next six months. It's important to keep our goals, hopes and dreams in bitesize chunks so we can actually make them happen.

Elaine said she'd like to work with wood and find her creative voice. Bravo! Now there's a dream that's doable. I hope she's enrolled in a woodworking class at a local community college by now.

Deborah's dream was to integrate her smarts and experience and talent into a position where she can make a difference in the world. Sounds like she could use the help of a good career counselor who can give her some integrated testing to find out where her strengths lie and what her options are.

Kitty wanted to visit Iceland, write about her travels and get her travelogues published. Knowing Kitty, she probably already had her plane ticket purchased.

Jean, who was in her mid seventies at the time, wanted to finish the eighth edition of a college textbook she wrote years ago and to keep her health in top shape by continuing her weight training and her three mile walks every day. Jean's dreams and goals kept the younger ones in our group inspired to the max.

Betty, a second grade teacher, said she wanted to leave a small mark on many lives. She emphasized that she didn't want the attention focused on her but rather on the lives she hoped to touch and change. As a teacher, Betty was living her dream every day.

Karen, who worked as a home health nurse, said her goal was to become a more positive influence at work. She said her work environment had become riddled with rumors and backbiting gossip and she wanted to be a catalyst for helping change the attitude and camaraderie on the job. She told us at the SWILL meeting that she was going to bring in a suggestion box where fellow employees would drop the funniest, most outrageous rumors they could think of. Karen had a good dream: to replace stress with laughter on the job.

Whitney, in her early twenties who was working on her PhD, said her goal was to facilitate a woman's group like SWILL someday to encourage and empower women. Right on!

Geri, a widow who remarried in her late sixties, said, "I'm living my dream, right now, every day. I'm happily married, have a new home and am recently retired. This is the happiest I've ever been."

What's your dream? What is it you're hoping for? Whether you're eighteen or ninety-eight, write it down and then get busy making it come true! Something to hope for is the most delicious of the five things we need to be happy. Hopes and dreams give our lives wings.

Following Dreams While We're Still Awake

Getting older is quite an adventure. Children leave home. Your body changes. Perky becomes saggy. Arthritis sets in. Jobs change or end. Friends move or die. Medical insurance costs hit the moon. Your eyesight gets worse. Your back aches.

Some of us in our midlife and golden years take it all in stride; others become lonely, fearful, bitter and depressed. I decided long ago to take the first path because I know that my happiness is one hundred percent dependent on me, not my kids, my family, my friends, my doctor or the work I do. I can either sit here crabby and lonely, moaning about growing older or I can do something to make myself happy.

I decided I needed a place in Florida where I could swim and bike to my heart's content year round. Yeah, right. Me, the single woman with the teeny income, winging her way through her seventeenth year of kids in college. Sure, a condo in Florida. I might as well have dreamed of a luxury liner picking me up on the shores of Lake Michigan and whisking me off to the Greek Isles where I could meet Zorba and dance the night away with a rose between my teeth.

But the problem is I'm a determined dreamer. So there I was, house-sitting for my dear friends Wally and Shirley in the middle of Florida's Pinellas County, nestled between Tampa Bay and the Gulf of Mexico, halfway between Clearwater Beach and St. Pete Beach, where a forty-nine-mile bike trail runs the length of the county. A safe, paved bike trail, ten feet wide and forty-nine miles long. Did I mention how much I like to bike?

That week I biked and swam during that house-sitting adventure in between my desperate dreaming and fanatical praying. *Lord, I don't ask you for specific things very often, but could you please help me find a way to have a place down here where it's warm in the winter, where the people are so friendly and where I can swim and bike to my heart's content? Thank you for considering it, Lord.*

The next day I phoned a realtor, mainly because it was raining and I was bored. She showed me a condo two blocks away on the third floor of what looked more like an apartment building than condo units. It had 1,100 square feet of space including a nice sun porch, two bedrooms and two baths. The amenities included a fabulous clubhouse and two beautiful swimming pools less than thirty yards from the building. The big heated pool was just three feet from the Intracoastal waterway and on the other side and across the street, the Gulf of Mexico. Paradise, for a swimmer like me. *Oh, Heavenly Father, it's just what I had in mind! Maybe in ten or fifteen years, Lord.*

I drooled, dreamed and gushed about the condo to my dad, my brother Joe and my sister Catherine. The next week after sending them photos of the condo, my brother flew down to check it out, and before I knew it, we all agreed to buy the place together, as a family. That was in April 2002. Then, for the next two years our four families visited paradise two, three or four times a year. We shared the condo and never had a squabble about anything. Sometimes we were together, sometimes we visited paradise alone or we'd bring other friends or relatives with us.

The ninety-five-year-old woman we bought it from left everything for us. All the furniture, small appliances, bedding, twenty-seven bath towels, two sets of dishes, pots, pans, everything. Not only that, but within a year and a half, the value of the place increased by at least twenty-five percent, which makes me feel better about spending most of my retirement money on my share.

Every time I visited our place in the sun, my heart not only sang, it did back flips. I could hardly believe that one dream of mine, that wild, crazy dream, actually came true the very month I started dreaming it.

Each time I visited our new family condo in Florida I biked every day, usually eight to fifteen miles, meandering through parks, then back on the forty-nine-mile-paved trail. My goal at one park that has a fresh water lake in the middle, was to spot an alligator in the water or sunning himself on the edge. Ninety percent of the time I saw one, admired it from a distance, shouted, "It's a great alligator day! Thank you, Lord!" then headed back to the bike trail for another hour of wonderful exercise.

I swam every day, sometimes twice. I loved it whether I was down there alone, meeting all sorts of fun-in-the-sun people who live in the neighborhood or whether I was with family or other friends from up north. I was living my dream.

I learned that even when I think something's impossible, it never is. I learned that when you pray very hard for something, often it comes true before you have time to turn around. I also learned that figuring out what our dreams are and then systematically going after them, is very, very important in the big scheme of things. If we don't dare to dream, even when we think we have no way to make those dreams come true, we will never experience the exquisite joy of following our dreams while we're still awake. Sometimes all it takes besides prayer is a little cooperation and communal effort from those you love the most.

Making Dreams Get Even Better

It wasn't long after my dream came true that I began to dream an even bigger one. The bigger dream took root when I started getting so excited each time a trip to Florida appeared on my horizon. The dream got bigger each time I noticed how sad and depressed I'd get whenever I had to go back home to cold Wisconsin. My kids were all grown and there I was living in a house that was much too large for me, with a yard big enough to require the services of a landscaper. Only I couldn't afford a landscaper.

I was doing a lot of professional speaking in those days and one of my favorite topics was *Follow Your Dreams While You're Still Awake.* I'd try to convince people to take stock of their lives, decide what's really important in the big scheme of things and then make drastic changes if necessary.

Sometimes I'd tell people the story of the flies that were kept in a small aerated jar. One day the lid was taken off the jar, but the flies just stayed inside, flying in circles exactly as they had done when the lid was on. They didn't even bother to fly out and discover the whole big world outside that jar. The jar had become their entire world. It happens to people too. Some of us are born, live and die in the same county or state and never get out of our small comfort zone to really experience all that life has to offer. Some of us dream big dreams but we never follow through.

After living for twenty-four years in that same house on the same street in Wisconsin, I decided to take my own advice and fly out of my jar, smack-dab into my bigger dream, the dream of actually living in a warm climate where I could swim every day all year long if I wanted to and where I'd never have to shovel snow off the driveway, salt sidewalks, wear three layers of clothes just to bring in the mail or fight weeds, trim trees or mow grass in my much-too-big-for-one-person yard.

One day, while relaxing by the pool in Florida during a vacation at our family condo, I simply did it. I made an offer on a condo, went home, sold my house and two-thirds of everything I owned and moved to Florida where the warm climate, sun, sand, sea, swimming pools and scintillating sunsets had lured me on vacations for years.

After the move I could hardly believe my life. The view from my office, sun porch and bedroom includes year-round greenery and flowers. Huge palm trees swaying in the Gulf breeze, large red hibiscus flowers blooming almost year-round, twenty-foot-tall red and white oleander bushes filled with flowers and other green bushes and flowering plants that make me gasp from their sheer beauty. It's all there, month after sunshiny month, even in the dead of winter. If the hope of this lifestyle made me happy, the fulfillment of the dream brought even more pure happiness.

From my kitchen and living/dining area I can see a sliver of the Intracoastal waterway, which is just three feet from the enormous heated pool I share with my neighbors, located right across the street from my new home. The Intracoastal entertains us with hundreds of boats sashaying down the waterway every week. Occasionally, two or three playful dolphins jump out of the water as they swim toward the Gulf. On the other side of the Intracoastal is one street, Gulf Boulevard, and then the magnificent Gulf of Mexico with its white sand beaches and waters so warm you can swim until mid-November in the eighty-something degree water.

This is my dream. A woman who loves to swim and bike. Did I mention the forty-nine-mile paved bike trail that runs the length of my new adopted county? Oh yes, of course I did, a few pages ago.

I have two friends with huge orange and grapefruit trees in their yards, so my favorite appliance has become my electric juicer. I've become a vitamin C freak. A woman thrilled out of my mind every morning when I wake up in what seems to be paradise and drink my fresh-squeezed orange juice. I'm convinced that the good Lord has never received so many prayers of gratitude from a single human before. It seems that every day, all day, I'm thanking God for something: my smaller, easier to clean, better organized condo; my fabulous new social life with more new friends than I've ever had; the fact that all winter long I never once turned on my furnace.

If there's a dream on your horizon, follow it. If not, get one. *Something to hope for* is a critical piece of the happiness puzzle. Maybe your dream is to move further north, out of the city. Perhaps you love the cold weather, snow, fireplaces, hot cocoa on a chilly evening. That's fine. Just do it. Don't wait until you're sixty, seventy or eighty to let your dreams come true. Change is more refreshing and more exciting than a gorgeous waterfall on a mountain slope. You say you're scared. You can't afford it. Your spouse would never want to move or join you in whatever your dream is. You think you're too old, your health is not that great or you wonder what your friends and family will think if your dream doesn't pan out the way you think it should. So what? It's *your* dream. *Your* life. Revise it a little, if necessary. Then go ahead and just do it.

Having *something to hope for* is a powerful ingredient for happiness. Start hoping and see what I mean.

Alice's Jubilee

On January 4, 1999, when my daughter Julia turned twenty-eight, she whined about her age. "I can't believe I'm this old!" she said wistfully. "I think I'm going to start counting backward. I'm telling everyone I'm twenty-six. In two years I'll be twenty-four."

I started thinking about the fact that Jeanne, my oldest daughter, would be thirty years old two weeks later. Then *I* started feeling old. How could I have a thirty-year-old daughter? Where did the years go?

Not long after that I received an invitation to my friend Alice's Jubilee. The invitation stated that on January 30, 1999, she would be celebrating her forty-ninth birthday, which to Alice meant that on that morning when she got out of bed she would be gloriously stepping into her fiftieth year . . . her Jubilee year. She invited over one hundred women friends to a hall for dinner and a program. More than seventy of us were able to attend.

The room was decorated with bright-colored balloons and flowers everywhere. After dinner, Alice talked with grace and deep appreciation about the women who had been the most influential in her life. There were hugs, tears, laughter and prayers. Then she darkened the room and lit a candle and as each woman in turn lit her candle from the woman next to her, we all mentioned one, two or three women who had been the most positive influential forces in our lives. Many mentioned their own mothers, favorite aunts or close friends. Others named famous women, poets, writers, politicians and Mother Teresa.

By the time I left Alice's Jubilee, I was so happy to be alive that I practically flew home on the tail of one of those brightly colored balloons. Alice had made each of us feel wise and cherished and, most of all, appreciative of the age we had attained.

A few months later Alice's friends received another invitation from her. This was to "Part Two" of the year-long celebration of her fiftieth year. This time eighteen women met in her living room to revel in the knowledge that we do indeed get better and wiser with age.

Alice passed out papers with five thought-provoking questions on them. *What chronological years would you define as midlife years? Where are you in your life journey? How are you doing physically, mentally, emotionally, spiritually at this point in your journey? What are your greatest fears about growing older? What is the best thing about growing older?*

We wrote down our answers and then chose a woman in the room to share with. The women, in pairs, scattered throughout Alice's apartment to discuss the answers, two by two. Val and I met on the steps and both shared that our biggest fear about growing older was that our health might decline. I also admitted my fear that the spiritual side of my being wouldn't develop enough in my lifetime to guarantee an A+ from the Almighty.

Next, Alice asked us to write down five significant events in our life and what those events had taught us about ourselves, others, God and life in general. The very act of writing down significant life-changing events was an exercise in profound soul searching.

Some of my significant events surprised me. Others didn't. My life-changing events included leaving home for college, giving birth to and raising four children, having the courage to get out of an abusive marriage, winning a major writing contest and starting a whole new career because of it, taking my youngest child to his father's funeral and learning, after breaking up with a wonderful man I'd dated for nearly three years, that it's okay to be single and that I am truly the only person responsible for my own happiness.

At Part Two of Alice's Jubilee, I learned that life truly is a journey of change and exciting things to hope for. I also learned that the process of becoming the complete person I was intended to be takes an entire lifetime. I learned that we're all still growing, whether we're thirty, fifty or seventy-five, and, as one of my favorite quotes says, "The destination will take care of itself if the journey is done well." (anonymous). We all know that half the fun of any journey is in the planning . . . the hope of exquisite days ahead. Having *something to hope for* brightens our happiness level and is both the whipped cream and the cherry on top of the sundae. Hope. It's the greatest gift ever.

Terrified on Timpanogos Mountain

During the summer of 1993, a good friend of mine, a widower named Wayne, my thirteen-year-old son Andrew and I took a four-week, six-thousand mile trip across America from Wisconsin to California and back. We had plenty of adventures but the most memorable happened on Timpanogos Mountain outside Salt Lake City, Utah.

On a warm, sunny July afternoon we chugged up Timpanogos Mountain to reach the place where you buy tickets for a cave tour near the top. A wooden sign warned:

> *To reach Timpanogos Cave, visitors must hike the 1.5 mile cave trail.*
>
> *This hard-surfaced trail rises 1,065 feet and is considered a strenuous hike.*
>
> *Anyone with heart trouble or walking or breathing problems should not attempt the hike. Allow three hours for the round trip, including an hour in the cave. Individuals under 16 must be directly supervised by an adult at all times.*

Since it was just 3:00 PM we had plenty of time before dark to walk up the trail, catch the last cave tour of the day and hike down. We bought our tickets and started to climb.

Even though we were in good shape, that trail was so steep we were huffing and puffing not long after we began. Every quarter mile or so we'd sit down on a bench to catch our breath. Enormous pines hundreds of feet below, sheer cliffs, rocks that stretched to the heavens and a clear blue sky that went on forever greeted us at every rest. Finally, after an hour of exhausting climbing we reached the entrance to the cave.

I plopped down on a bench just inside the cave entrance next to an older man wearing a beige one-piece worksuit and a miner's hat with a light attached. I tried to make conversation but the older man looked at me as if he didn't understand what I was saying. Finally he spoke in a very thick Spanish accent, telling me that it had taken him over two-and-a-half hours to climb up the mountain. He was exhausted and upset that he'd missed the scheduled time for his tour. His name was Emilio and he was originally from Madrid. He was seventy years old and said he had no idea how steep the climb would be.

Then our tour guide appeared. She welcomed Emilio into our group and opened the door to the cave. An hour and a half later, after exploring the beautiful winding Timpanogos Cave, we stepped back into daylight. Only it wasn't bright and sunny anymore. It was cloudy, windy and starting to sprinkle.

Andrew didn't like the looks of it one bit.

"Mom, hurry up, it's raining. We gotta get down. It could be a big storm."

I glanced behind me toward the cave exit, wondering what was taking Emilio so long. I stalled by signing our names on the guest register. I can't explain why I couldn't leave other than to say that a voice inside my head said I needed to wait for Emilio.

"Mom! Come on! Look how windy it's getting! We gotta get down!" Andrew was starting to panic.

"Andrew, wait a minute. Emilio's right behind us."

"Who cares? Mom, it's really starting to rain! Let's go!"

I had no idea what was ahead of us or why I couldn't leave without the old man, but that inner voice would not let me leave until Emilio was safely out of the cave and walking with us.

I tried to reason with Andrew. "It's going to take us at least an hour to get down, maybe longer. We're going to get wet no matter what. Let's just wait for him."

"Mom, do you see those black clouds over Salt Lake City in the distance? That's rain pouring out of them! And they're moving this way! It's getting darker!"

I could see my son was really scared. I certainly didn't like what

I saw ahead of us either. A steep, narrow, mountain path with no guard rail was *not* where I wanted to be during a thunderstorm.

Just then Emilio stepped out of the cave. Andrew skittered down the first leg of the switchback path. I walked slowly, just ahead of Emilio. Within a few minutes Andrew had disappeared around the first sharp turn.

"Mom! Hurry up!" Andrew yelled. "I can see lightning in the distance!"

Right then a giant sharp cracking noise slammed into the mountain. It wasn't the rolling thunder I was used to in Wisconsin. This sounded like ten thousand bullwhips had snapped right in front of us into the side of the rock, a nasty heart-stopping sound. Then a giant rod of white light zigzagged just ahead of us.

"Mom!" Andrew screamed. "Hurry up!" I knew my son wanted to run and not stop until he reached the bottom where the car was.

The wind roared and I crouched behind a rock outcrop. As the sky turned black, the clouds let loose and the pouring rain and wind began. Stones and small rocks flew off the mountain and smashed at our feet. I could feel my heart slamming against my chest. I closed my eyes tight and prayed as more lightning flashed in front of us.

"Ouch!" Andrew let out a yelp. "Mom, I just got hit in the head by a rock the size of a baseball! Can't you go any faster?"

I couldn't move. I started praying again. *God, don't let us die out here. Protect us and keep Emilio's legs strong.*

For the first time in my life I honestly thought I might die. I thought we would all die. *Maybe it's our time,* I reasoned. I figured at best we'd get struck by lightning and die instantly. At worst the wind would blow us off the path and we'd plunge down the steep rocky thousand-foot drop to the valley below.

Andrew tried to cover his eyes from the thick dust blowing around our heads by pulling his baseball cap farther down on his head as the rain soaked his T-shirt. As he crouched down to wait for me I pulled my reading glasses out of my pocket and put them on to keep the dust from blowing in my eyes. I shouted over the wind, "Stay calm, Andrew. We'll be okay."

Another giant crack. This one sounded like the mountain itself had split in half. Then more lightning, closer this time.

Andrew and Wayne were fifty feet ahead of Emilio and me. There were places on the path that had a blue line painted down the middle. A sign said that when you saw a blue line you were supposed to walk fast because those were the areas where rock slides were likely to occur. Andrew and Wayne were on one side of a rock slide area and Emilio and I were on the other.

I was shivering as cold rain ran down my neck. Finally, I looked up to make sure no large rocks were falling and raced across the blue line section and caught up to my son.

"We have to wait for Emilio," I said matter-of-factly.

"Why, Mom? He can make it by himself. He got up here, didn't he? I don't like this. Let me go by myself. You know how long it took Emilio to get up this mountain! I can't stand this!"

I put my hands on Andrew's shoulders. "Andrew, please. He's not very strong. He just told me he was in the hospital last summer with an ulcerated pancreas. His knees hurt him. It's harder walking down this mountain than it was going up. I'm using muscles I've never used before to keep from falling on my face! And now the path is wet and slippery. It's covered with rocks and there's no guard rail."

Crack! Another thunderclap and a bolt of lightning followed almost immediately. I took a deep breath and grabbed a tree root sticking out of the side of the mountain.

"What? I can't hear you!" Andrew shouted hysterically.

I yelled over the howling wind, "Andrew, think of all the things that could happen to Emilio. He could lose his balance and slip on a rock. He could have a heart attack from exhaustion. He..."

Andrew pulled away from me and interrupted. "Okay, Okay! Geez, Mom, this is going to take forever!" He wasn't happy but I think he was starting to understand.

"Wait, Andrew, I'm not finished."

My son rolled his eyes, expecting a lecture. I put my hands back on his shoulders. Suddenly, once again, a voice spoke inside my head, *Use Andrew's shoulders.*

"Andrew, you're strong. I can feel it in your shoulders. You're five feet, nine inches, a little shorter than Emilio. How would you feel about letting him put his hands on your shoulders from behind for support?"

I looked back up the path at Emilio. I could see clumps of wet white hair under the child-size miner's cap he'd purchased earlier that day in the gift shop below. He was bent over, hands on his knees, panting for breath. I looked at the dark clouds. It was still raining and the path was sloppy wet and slippery. Andrew was looking at him too . . . then at the black clouds, at the bent trees blowing wildly in the wind and then back at Emilio.

Then his voice softened. "Okay, Mom, I'll do it."

Emilio liked the idea of using Andrew's shoulders for support as the two of them baby-stepped down the path as the rain pelted their backs. Shuffle, rest. Shuffle, rest. Emilio could only take twenty or so steps before he had to lean against the mountain and rest his knees.

As we shuffled along with me in the front pushing rocks off the wet path and Emilio's hands on Andrew's shoulders and Wayne bringing up the rear, we looked like the blind leading the blind. Andrew thought we looked so funny that he started whistling the song from *Bridge on the River Kwai* where the prisoners did their single-file death march. In a few seconds Emilio and I were whistling along with him.

Then Emilio started teaching Andrew Spanish. "*Esta es una montana grand! Vamonos amigos!*" He'd say phrases in Spanish and Andrew would repeat them.

Next he told Andrew tales about his life in Madrid, about his Cuban wife, how he'd lived in New York for many years and the three years he worked as an auditor on a Norwegian ship.

As I walked ahead kicking stones and rocks out of the path, I could tell from Andrew's comments and questions that he was genuinely starting to like this old guy. Even when they had to stop every few minutes to give Emilio's knees another rest, they joked back and forth until we'd hear Emilio's loud voice echo through the mountains, "Vamonos muchachos!"

After an hour the black clouds moved further south. Our slow procession continued as the pounding rain gradually slowed to a drizzle. For three-and-a-half hours, as we inched our way down that steep, slippery mountain path, Emilio and Andrew were glued to each other, Emilio's hands on Andrew's shoulders.

Ten feet before we reached the bottom, Emilio pulled away from my son and stood tall by himself. In his loud, clear voice with the thick Spanish accent he proclaimed, "I do the last steps myself! So, Andrew, when we reach the bottom shall we purchase the tickets to do this again tomorrow?" he laughed.

We all laughed. When Emilio reached level ground we cheered. I gave him a hug and we walked him to his car in the dark of night. By now it was after 9:30 PM and our two cars were the only ones left in the parking lot.

Before he opened his car door Emilio shook my son's hand and said, "Andrew, you are a fine young man. I could not have made it down without your help. Thank you."

Later, as we drove back to Salt Lake City, Andrew said he felt sad when Emilio drove away. He said he wanted to talk to him some more, that he wanted to hear his big belly laugh again.

I asked Andrew if he'd learned anything special that day. He thought for a minute, then smiled.

"Yup. I learned that when you help somebody you forget your own fears. As soon as Emilio put his hands on my shoulders, I wasn't afraid of the storm any more. I also learned that God definitely answers your prayers. When we weren't talking or whistling, I was praying . . . a lot."

Sometimes having *something to hope for* means great bursts of hope that we'll survive a scary situation. But even in a situation like that, we feel alive, exuberant. After the violent storm passed and as we continued to march slowly down that mountain in the rain, I was almost giddy with excitement. I watched my son escape his fears by giving his time and care to an old man. Believe me, to see a thirteen year old son do something like this creates a kind of happiness inside a mother that's hard to beat.

Bringing It to Pass, Football and All

Hope comes in all sizes and flavors. Hope is all entwined in our dreams, expectations, wishes and goals of life. Looking forward to something takes us out of the present and snaps up right into the future where we hope things will be better, different, more exciting, more fun, rewarding or surrounded with a gentler, kinder clientele or atmosphere. And it usually is.

Hope is the stuff of great happiness. As a mother I learned firsthand with all four of my children that it's the anticipation of the holiday, the birthday, the trip, the adventure that is usually much more fun than that actual event itself. Anticipation makes us all tingly inside. We wonder, watch, wait. What's it going to be like? What will I do when I get there? How will my life change when I get that new job? What will my new friends be like when I move?

Anticipation is delicious. Sometimes it's scary, like waiting for that roller-coaster ride. But it's a good kind of scary.

I remember one great adventure I had that was all wrapped up in anticipation. *Something to hope for.* It started one crisp fall day in Madison, Wisconsin, in 1994 when our University of Wisconsin football team defeated the University of Illinois in the final Big Ten Conference home game of the season. The win guaranteed Wisconsin a chance to play in a postseason Holiday Bowl game for the second year in a row. The previous year Wisconsin had won the Big Ten championship and had gone on to defeat the UCLA Bruins at the Rose Bowl in Pasadena.

Now Wisconsin was headed to the Hall of Fame Bowl in Tampa, Florida, over the Christmas holidays. My twenty-two-year-old son Michael, a senior at the University of Wisconsin was a four-year member of their marching band, famous for their wildly entertaining high-stepping antics that dazzle crowds at every pregame, halftime and the band's famous *fifth quarter* after each game.

I'd desperately wanted to go to the Rose Bowl game the previous New Year's to watch my son perform, but the trip was too expensive. I didn't know anyone in Pasadena to stay with and airfare was out of the question. So, on New Year's Day 1994 my house was full of relatives as we all watched Michael on TV. He played his drums with such precision during the Rose Bowl parade and game that my heart nearly burst with excitement and pride.

But when the Wisconsin Badgers won the right to play in the Hall of Fame Bowl the very next season, I realized that that game would be Michael's last time ever to march with the band before he graduated . . . my son's last hurrah, so to speak. After four of the most exciting years of his life, I just *had* to be there.

Right. A single parent with a small income and bigger-than-life dreams. That was me.

In late November I mentioned my dream to my airline pilot friends who used the extra bedrooms in our home as their Milwaukee-area home away from home. One said he had a couple of low-cost airline passes left for the year that my fifteen-year-old son Andrew and I could use to get to Tampa and back.

"The passes are only about ninety dollars each, round-trip, but you'll have to fly standby," he warned.

I jumped at the chance as he set things in motion. Next, I had to find housing. I looked on the map and saw that our retired friends, Wally and Shirley, live just forty-five minutes from Tampa. I was sure they'd put us up for the week in their Florida condo.

Everything seemed to be working smoothly until I called my dad in Illinois to tell him the good news. Dad planted my feet back on the ground when he said, "You're going to Florida between Christmas and New Year's? That's the busiest tourist week of the year down there. And you're flying standby? What do you think your chances are of getting on a plane that week?"

My bubble of optimism burst in midair once again when I heard on the radio that nearly thirty thousand Wisconsinites had already bought tickets to the Hall of Fame Bowl to see their Badgers play the Duke Blue Devils in Tampa. If you've ever been to Wisconsin in the winter, you can understand why so many people were jumping at the chance to go to a warmer climate for few days in December and January. Our chances of getting down there flying standby certainly didn't look good. They looked impossible, in fact. But I could still hope, right?

However, there was another glitch in the plans. The Milwaukee-based airline we'd be flying on only had one flight a day to Tampa. How could I even think there'd be empty seats on that plane during the week between Christmas and New Year's?

I told myself disgustedly, *How could you be so stupid? This will never work.*

In addition to decorating for Christmas, buying gifts, cleaning house, and planning meals for my older children, son-in-law, and granddaughter who would be coming home for Christmas, I now had an additional stressor in my life. How could we possibly get to Florida?

I talked to my friend Heather. Before Heather and her husband Rusty moved to our home town the previous summer, Rusty had been one of my houseguest pilots for four months.

"Heather, I already bought four Hall of Fame Bowl tickets so Andrew and I and our friends in Florida can see Michael march in his last game. The tickets cost me one hundred twenty dollars! And we stand about as much chance of getting on that plane the last week of December as Tampa has of having a two-foot snowfall during the game. What was I thinking?"

Heather smiled and grabbed my hand. "Pat. Stop worrying. Do something for me. Look through the book of Psalms. Read it until you find a verse that seems to be speaking to you."

I looked at Heather as if she'd just told me to go plant a grapefruit tree in my snow-filled backyard.

"Psalms? What am I going to find in there?" I asked Heather.

"Just do it. You'll find what you're looking for."

That afternoon I opened my Bible and read the first two psalms. Nothing hit me. The third verse said something about *bearing luscious fruit each season without fail,* which only depressed me more because it made me think of ruby red grapefruit and large juicy oranges hanging on trees all over Florida, fruit that I certainly wouldn't be enjoying.

This can't be the verse that's supposed to make me feel better, I thought. I closed the book and opened it again at random. This time my eyes went directly to Psalms 37:5.

> *Commit thy way unto the Lord: trust also in him; and he shall bring it to pass.* (KJV)

Two things about that verse nearly threw me for a loop. The part about committing my *way* to the Lord . . . my *way* to see my son perform in his last game, perhaps? The other was the notion that the Lord would bring it to pass. If I did my part that was God's promise. If I really, truly *trusted* in the Lord, then He would bring it to pass. Also, I have to admit that the word *pass* was a clincher since Andrew and I would be flying standby on airline companion *passes*.

Okay, Patricia, this is it. If Heather can be so dead-bolt certain of her faith, why can't you? You have to put it on the line. Do you truly believe that this is in the hands of the Lord and that He will bring it to pass?

I only had to ask myself that question once. I sat down that moment and memorized verse 37:5. And if you want to know the truth, it was the first Bible verse I'd ever memorized in my life. I've been a longtime Bible reader and studier, but memorizing is very difficult for me.

But I memorized *Commit thy way unto the Lord; trust also in him; and he shall bring it to pass.* Not only did I memorize it, but I said it at least a hundred times a day during those weeks before Christmas.

The minute I turned the problem over to the Lord, I relaxed completely and virtually sailed through the preparations for Christmas. Never again did I worry about whether or not we'd get on the plane.

One night, Eric, one of the pilots staying at my house, called the airline's reservations desk and asked for the exact number of tickets that had been sold for those few flights to Tampa during Christmas week. Every flight had been greatly oversold with the exception of Christmas morning. And even for that flight eighty of the eightyfour seats had been sold, with three weeks still to go before Christmas.

Eric shook his head. "I'm sorry, Pat. Wish I could do something to help."

"Well, that's where this trust thing is going to work, Eric," I told my houseguest. "I'm stepping out in faith, ready to march, just like Michael's marching band. I'm trusting in the Lord. We're getting on that plane; I just know it."

Eric smiled and shook his head, no doubt figuring I had a screw loose somewhere. Or perhaps he was just surprised that I'd suddenly become so verbal about my faith.

For the next three weeks I repeated my newly memorized verse a thousand times. Before I got out of bed in the morning, before each meal, during the day, in the car, in my home office, walking down the hall, in bed at night. I repeated it to all my friends and family and assured them that Andrew and I would be in Tampa for the Hall of Fame Bowl on January 2, and that we'd be flying down there on Christmas morning. Hope reigned supreme.

Christmas Eve day dawned holy and cold in Milwaukee. My grown children, son-in-law, granddaughter, friends Rusty and Heather and their two little daughters, Andrew and I all celebrated Christ's birth at our Christmas Eve dinner amidst my giggling excitement as I packed our bags for Florida. I shared my memorized Bible verse from Psalms with them as part of the grace before dinner.

"So, Mom, are you just going to keep going back to the airport every day all week until you get on a plane?" my daughter Julia asked during dessert.

"No honey, we'll be getting on the plane tomorrow morning. I'll send you postcards and bring you seashells!"

Never before in my life had I been so sure of something, something that to all the sensible people around me seemed to be the folly of the century.

Bags packed, car loaded, Michael drove us to the airport at 7:30 AM, Christmas Day. The gate agent said there'd been four people with emergencies in Florida, and they'd been given priority standby status. It didn't matter. I knew that when that gate closed we'd be on that plane.

That afternoon Andrew and I picked grapefruit from the tree next to the hot tub in the backyard of our friends' house in Florida, as we celebrated Christmas with new friends and old. Nine days later, after sunning ourselves on Gulf beaches, exploring exotic wonders, and following the Wisconsin marching band as they performed all over Tampa, we watched as the University of Wisconsin defeated the Duke Blue Devils in the Hall of Fame Bowl on a beautiful, sunny, eighty-degree day.

Michael's last performance with the band was stellar. But not quite as stellar as my faith in the Lord who brings all things to pass . . . if we just put our trust in Him, relax and hope like crazy. *Something to hope for.* It's downright magical.

Chapter Five

Something to Believe In

One person with a belief is equal to a force of ninety-nine who only have interest.

—*John Stuart Mill*

Something to believe in is critical in this happiness puzzle because it gives wings to all those things we simply can't understand or explain. But most of all, having something to believe in is a gigantic comfort. Faith is a gift. Some have the gift, some don't. It isn't our job to decide who does and who doesn't. And certainly it's not up to us to say who's going to heaven and who isn't. Personally, I don't think God put anyone on this earth to judge others. *Something to believe in*, like happiness itself, must come from within.

Life after Death

Ever have one of those months or years when it seems the whole world, or at least your little section of it, is falling apart? As in, everybody you know is sick, was just diagnosed with a disease, or is in the last stages of life? We all go through it.

I remember one particularly rough time when a number of friends were experiencing more than their share of tough stuff. First my friend Sharon got leukemia. During the time when she was really sick from double doses of chemo her husband got pneumonia. At the same time her college-age daughter was sick with strep throat. *How much can one family endure,* I wondered?

Two other friends were battling cancer, one in the last stages. One friend was having test after test because the doctor thought she either had MS or a brain tumor. My daughter-in-law's mother finished chemo for breast cancer and a few months later found another lump. A writer friend of mine said her doctor had found a mass on her spleen.

All this did a number on my life in two ways. First, my prayer time increased by hours, and second, I started thinking about death. What does it mean? Why do some of us have to suffer more than others? What's it like when we die?

As I prayed and pondered my friend Diane told me that her best friend's daughter had died suddenly, a twenty-seven-year-old mother of two. Diane was asked to give the eulogy, a task she wasn't sure she was up to.

"Any ideas?" Diane asked.

For some reason all I could think about was something Jerry Seinfeld once said. "The number-one fear people have is public speaking. The number-two fear is death. Therefore if you're ever asked to give a eulogy, you're actually worse off than the person in the casket."

I knew that wouldn't help Diane, so I decided to rewrite an old story I'd heard a long time ago. I don't know if Diane used it in her eulogy or not, but if you're having a time like I did when so many friends seem to be seriously ill or even dying, I hope this helps.

In a huge field there lived a colony of caterpillars. Caterpillars Omar and Gloria were talking one day. Omar said, "Have you ever noticed that various members of our clan climb up these tall milkweed stalks, hide from us on top of the biggest leaves, and then disappear from sight forever?"

Gloria wiggled her fuzzy little body and exclaimed, "Yes, just the other day, old Oscar got to the top of one of those leaves and I haven't seen him since. I wonder where they all go. And why don't they come back?"

Omar continued, "Well, let's promise each other that if we ever climb to the top of one of the milkweed stalks and disappear that we'll come back and tell the other one what was so great that we gave up our old life down here on the ground."

About a week later Gloria decided to climb up a five-foot-tall milkweed stalk. When she reached the top and was out of sight of the others on the ground, she began to change. The hair disappeared on her body, her six legs got longer and more graceful and two lovely antennas emerged from her head. Now she was able to taste magnificent sweet nectars for the first time. Finally, four large, iridescent multicolored wings emerged from her back. Gloria, the butterfly, pushed off from the tip of the milkweed stalk and took flight, doing *loop-de-loops among the neighboring flower fields in the bright sunny sky for the rest of the day.*

At nightfall she remembered her promise to Omar but as she swooped in and out of the milkweed stalks she couldn't find him. And with her beautiful new wings and totally different look, she knew that Omar would never recognize her anyway.

"Oh well, at least I tried," she said wistfully as she fluttered around a mighty oak tree surrounded by wild flowers and then sailed off to discover more of the amazing paradise before her.

"I guess Omar and the rest of them will just have to wait until they climb up the milkweed stalks and change into butterflies before they will understand how incredible it is up here."

Isn't that what death is all about? Don't we become totally different, so different that no one here on earth can even imagine what happens when we die?

Next time you're missing a loved one who has died, just remember that he or she has become something new, something so totally wonderful and amazing that we can't even begin to comprehend it here on earth. Just know that it is good, that the freedom is totally delicious and that he or she has reached perfection. When we believe in a glorious life after death, really truly believe, the anguish we feel when a loved one dies can be soothed by our belief. *Something to believe in* makes the pain go away.

A Lesson from the Dolphins

SOMETHING TO BELIEVE IN is out there for us, just for the asking. Sometimes we find it in the strangest places, when we're so far removed from anything even remotely religious. Faith is a gift. Like talent, it's something that we don't work for, deserve, plan for or buy. It's there, inside us all, for the taking, a true gift. Some accept the gift, others don't. All I know is that when you do have *something to believe in*, your stress levels go way down, your happiness quotient soars and life is a lot easier. At least that's how it's always worked for me. I figure life is just too short to spend it stressed out or fretting about much of anything and when things start to go haywire in my life, I just turn it all over to God. My faith kicks in and my worry meter goes down.

I was born into faith. A lifelong Catholic father and a Protestant-turned-Catholic mother. Educated by nuns, the wonderful Sisters of Loretto, for fourteen years including my first two years of college. Faith came easy to me. I was born again into the world of faith in God and Jesus Christ on the day of my Baptism while still an infant and have treasured my gift of faith ever since. I've known all my life that faith is what propelled me through the rough times and made the easy times more joyous.

I remember one particular year, 1995, the year I would turn fifty. I was definitely not looking forward to that fiftieth birthday until my oldest daughter Jeanne called from California.

"Mom, you're supposed to do *Hawaii 5-0* when you turn fifty.

It's a tradition. I'll pay your airfare. I'm taking you to Hawaii next summer for your birthday."

The day before my fifteen-year-old son Andrew and I left to join Jeanne and her boyfriend Canyon on our adventure of a lifetime, I received a letter from Social Security.

"I don't understand this, " I blubbered to the representative on the phone after I tore open the letter.

She responded kindly, "If a minor child only has one living parent, that parent receives financial help from social security until the child is sixteen. The child continues to receive it until he's eighteen, however."

I hung up the phone in a daze. In four months, one-third of my annual income would be gone.

Well, it was too late to cancel the vacation. Jeanne was eagerly awaiting our arrival in California. And besides, I'd saved like the dickens for six months to pay for Andrew's airfare and the rest of the trip. So, instead of worrying about the future, I repeated my favorite Bible verse over and over. *Commit thy way unto the Lord; trust also in him; and he shall bring it to pass.* (Psalms 37:5, KJV)

The August vacation was spectacular, but when I returned home and started thinking about how my financial future was in a downward spiral, my approaching-fifty body decided to have its own heyday.

First, a huge portion of my back tooth broke into little pieces. When the crown was put in I had to fork over $487 to my dentist. No dental insurance, of course.

The next day I received a bill for X-rays I'd had before the trip of my arthritic toe . . . $144. The meager medical insurance I could afford didn't cover X-rays.

That same week I noticed I was having trouble reading the fine print and sometimes even the medium print. Out of desperation I purchased a huge light for the kitchen that contained four four-foot-long fluorescent bulbs. It made cooking, bill paying, reading and letter writing at the kitchen counter much easier for my approaching-fifty eyes. But that new light set me back $107.

Next, I made a trip to the optometrist's office. He said both my distance and close-up vision were worse.

Naturally, I thought bitterly, as my whole physical well-being flashed before my eyes in bright neon. It said, *You're almost fifty. Over the hill.*

The bill for the new bifocals and reading glasses was $241.

That same week, I finally gave in to one too many backaches caused by the ancient desk chair in my home office. I figured that the lower back pain was just another *old-age* pitfall.

But once again, I repeated my favorite verse from Psalms, stepped out in faith and wrote out a check for $105 for a superb office chair with arms and lumbar support. The day after I put that chair together I noticed a great improvement in my back.

Well now, at least my broken tooth was fixed, I could see near and far with my new glasses, my back didn't hurt and my arthritic toe felt better after all the hiking I did in Hawaii. Physically, things seemed to be looking up. But financially, things were out of control. First my income was going down by a third, then all those bills. I wasn't just going over the hill agewise, I was careering down financially as well as physically.

And so I prayed. "Thank you, Lord, for providing for my son and me." Of course, I ended the prayer with my favorite verse from Psalms. I firmly believed that if I truly trusted the Lord, I had to do just that . . . trust him to take care of us. But I still wasn't happy about turning fifty.

The next week, as my real birthday in October loomed closer, I started putting my photo album together from the trip to Hawaii. I looked at us sitting in kayaks and recalled the most exciting day we'd had on the big island.

On the morning of Day Twelve we'd rented ocean kayaks and paddled a mile or so to the most spectacular snorkeling spot on the big island. The Technicolor fish and amazing coral filled our underwater day with awe. Late in the afternoon as we started back across the bay to return the rented kayaks, we lollygagged across the calm, crystal clear ocean water snuggled into the rim of a beautiful treelined bay.

Suddenly huge fish were popping out of the water just ahead of us. Fish? They were dolphins! Dozens of them, at least eighty or a hundred. We paddled like crazy to get closer, then the four of us sat in stunned silence when we reached the spot where the dolphins were playing. As we sat motionless in that great ocean those dolphins jumped out of the water, did spins and flips in the air, dove in perfect unison four or five across and entertained us all around our two kayaks. They seemed as happy to see us as we them and for twenty minutes we four were spellbound.

Canyon spoke first, almost in a whisper. "This is a God-moment. We'll never forget this as long as we live."

I nodded as six sleek dolphins, in perfect synchronization, jumped out of the water, then glided within feet of the kayak Andrew and I were in.

As I tucked photos of Hawaiian beaches, sunsets and volcanoes into my album I thought about what Canyon had said.

A God-moment, I mused. Perhaps my life at this junction of turning fifty is a God-moment. Could it be that turning fifty means a new freedom, a chance to swim and dance and spin with the same glee and abandonment that the dolphins demonstrated?

It's true, I thought, those magnificent creatures had plenty of worries of their own, like where the next couple hundred fish would come from for dinner that night, and how to protect their young from sharks and other predators. And yet there they were, a hundred of them, playing and entertaining us with complete, joyful abandonment, in the environment that God had provided.

Unknowingly, perhaps, those dolphins had *committed their way to the Lord* and were enjoying their very existence to the fullest. Why couldn't I do the same?

Right then I decided to *work smarter* a few extra hours in my home office each day until I could get all those "getting-older" medical bills paid off.

I made a promise to myself not to buy any clothing or unneeded household items for three years. After all, I had plenty of clothes and if I just stayed out of the stores, I'd resist impulse buying.

Next, I made a list of all the things I could do with my life after Andrew, my youngest, went to college. I could teach workshops in various parts of the country. Write books. Visit more friends and relatives. Sleep longer in the mornings, stay up later at night. Eat when I feel like it. Take more bike rides. Make new friends.

Suddenly I felt as free as one of those dolphins in the balmy Pacific Ocean. My faith tells me that the Lord does take care of all his creatures, great and small, dolphins and damsels. And whether I'm thirty, fifty or ninety, there's plenty waiting for me on the horizon, no matter what decade I'm in. Having *something to believe in,* a wonderful God who answers prayers, sometimes in ways I don't understand, makes me happy. It just does.

Love Those Struggles

Everyone has struggles. Everyone. Some have tougher struggles than others, but no life is perfect. One guy who had lots of struggles once said, "You will never be a winner unless you learn to be a loser." He should know. He was a big loser. In his early years after a difficult childhood and less than one year of formal schooling he failed in business. What did he expect, with no education? Then he actually had the nerve to run for the state legislature. He was defeated, of course. Then, the next year he failed in another business venture. No surprise there. The following year, believe it or not, he was elected to the legislature. One thing's for sure, the guy had persistence. The next year his beloved fiancée died. Heartbroken, his struggles continued. Three years later, he was defeated for speaker of the house, then defeated for elector. Defeat after defeat seemed to follow him like a ruthless black cloud that precedes the rain.

Finally the man got married, but his wife suffered from numerous ailments both mental and physical. Living with her was a daily high-maintenance struggle, but even so, they had four sons. The sad thing is that only one of his four sons lived past the age of eighteen. Thirteen years after he got married he was defeated when he ran for Congress. You'd think the guy would give up, right? But the thing is, he loved politics and was determined to move ahead. So he persisted and five years later he was finally elected to Congress. However, seven years later he was defeated when he ran for Senate. Then this man, whose life was one giant struggle after another, actually had the nerve to run for Vice President of the United States, but, of course, he was defeated. Two years later, he lost in the Senate race, again. Did he finally give it up and accept the fact that he was a big-time loser? No. As unbelievable as it sounds he actually ran for President two years after losing his second election to the Senate. And, get this . . . he won!

This man, who struggled for years and years with poverty, an unhappy marriage, the death of most of his children and losing election after election after election, went on to become one of the greatest presidents the United States has ever known. Abraham Lincoln had learned firsthand that "you will never be a winner unless you learn to be a loser."

What kept him going? Faith. He had *something to believe in.* He knew God had given him the gift to be a leader and he stumbled over rocks, boulders and mountains until he reached the potential God had in store for him. He believed in the gift God gave him. His faith provided the armor he needed to keep going in life.

I remember the first time I felt like a loser. I was eleven years old, in the sixth grade. My cousin Judy, also eleven, was in the same class. Our last names were both Kobbeman, since our dads were brothers. That year Judy and I tied for the third place academic award, but the small Catholic school we attended only had one third place certificate to give out. They gave it to her because her first name, Judy, came before mine, Patricia, in the alphabet. I was devastated. But I learned a valuable lesson. I learned that life isn't fair, but you go on anyway. I learned that living through struggles and disappointments gives you strength of character.

I felt like a big loser thirty years later when my second husband filed for divorce and then married his girlfriend the day the divorce was final. Once again, I learned a valuable lesson that relationships, no matter how busy you are with children, career and home, must be nurtured every single day and that we can never take those we love for granted.

Learning to appreciate and grow from our struggles is a sign of maturity. One of my favorite stories is about a young woman who met a very wise old woman. The young woman asked, "How did you get so wise?" The old woman replied slowly with two words: "Good decisions." The young woman asked, "How did you learn to make good decisions?" The old woman replied with one word: "Experience." The young woman asked, "But how did you get experience?" The old woman replied with two words, "Bad decisions."

And so it is that our bad decisions, our defeats and our struggles eventually make us strong. They make us more mature. They certainly make us more interesting than if we lived a perfect life in perfect harmony on Perfect Lane in a perfect home with a perfect white picket fence. Our struggles give us strength of character and they help us to become much more empathetic toward all those around us who have struggles and problems too.

If you're struggling with a faltering career, an unhappy marriage, the loss of a loved one, lack of money, low self-esteem, poor health, whatever it is, remind yourself that true happiness does not come from a big paycheck and the so-called perfect life. True happiness comes from knowing that you have *something to believe in* and therefore there is something good ahead waiting for you. True happiness comes from your climb out of the pit. True happiness and contentment come because of the many struggles we experience in life. For without them none of us would have the fine patina of experience, growth, strength and compassion.

A Gathering of the Clan

When Aunt Mary Kobbeman, age eighty-five, died in February 2000, I drove to my hometown, Rock Falls, Illinois, to attend the funeral. Luckily, I'd been home just three weeks earlier and visited Aunt Mary in the hospital. I did my grieving during and after that visit. Aunt Mary was not happy. Her body was a withered pain-filled shell of her former vibrant self. Her laughing, dancing days were over and life was reduced to short visits with her children and grandchildren and begging for a drink of water as she plodded listlessly through her fluid-restricted diet.

The week before she died Aunt Mary slipped and broke her hip. After surgery, the Bishop of the Rockford diocese, who happened to be in town for Catholic schools week, stopped in to see Aunt Mary at the hospital, thanks to his friendship with her son, Father Jerry, who at the time was the pastor of a large church in Aurora, Illinois. She died peacefully two days later.

Aunt Mary's wake was in a word, fun. I mean really fun! Seven of her eleven children (two preceded her in death and two could not make it from the west coast for various reasons) and their spouses took their positions at the front of the large room in the funeral home. I stood near the front myself as one of the cousins who spent much of my childhood at Aunt Mary's farm. As friends and other relatives filed by, we hugged, talked, laughed and told stories. It was a visitation that made proud the word visit. For four hours we cousins jabbered with dozens of old friends and relatives we hadn't seen for years about Aunt Mary and her remarkable years as a single parent raising eleven children alone on a farm in northern Illinois. Uncle Harry had been killed in a farm accident when the youngest was six months old and the oldest nineteen. Aunt Mary went back to college, got her teaching degree and taught fourth grade for years in order to keep her kids fed, clothed and the farm running as smooth as possible.

Aunt Mary's kids and I giggled about our days on the farm. We talked about Queeny, the too-fat, too-slow horse. About the elaborate tunnels we used to make upstairs in the barn with hundreds and hundreds of bales of hay. About looking for tadpoles in the ditch alongside the farmhouse. About the baseball games and rowdy dinners we cousins enjoyed together with Aunt Mary at the helm.

The next day the fun continued at Aunt Mary's funeral. My

folks and I arrived early and joined in the hug fest in the vestibule of the church. More chatter and laughter continued as Father Jerry orchestrated the event including the arrival of forty-five priests, the Bishop and the Bishop emeritus. When I saw what kind of a send-off the mother of a priest gets, I made a mental note to talk to my unmarried son about a possible vocation to the priesthood. (An idea that didn't take, by the way.)

After the funeral, our huge family reunion continued in the school cafeteria where we cousins had eaten every noon meal in grade school. We told more stories, laughed until our sides hurt, traded desserts and photos of our kids. During that lunch we recalled the unbending persistence and fortitude it took Aunt Mary to raise eleven kids alone in the 1960s and 1970s.

After lunch, dozens of cars lined up for the ten-mile parade to the cemetery next to the little country church in Tampico, Illinois, where most of the other family members are buried. After the graveside service in the bitter cold where the siblings and we cousins, aunts and uncles huddled together, arms linked in love and protection from the cold, we were treated to coffee and desserts in the hall of the little country church. Again, for the fourth time in two days, we friends and relatives carried on the tradition of having more fun than should be legally permitted at a funeral. But we weren't there to cry, express regrets or to be sad.

We were there to celebrate. We celebrated Aunt Mary's zest for living and her devotion to her family. We celebrated life. I am just glad to be part of a faith and a family where the send-offs can be as much fun as family reunions. Without a doubt, *something to believe in*, gives wings to despair . . . wings that create total, unabashed happiness.

Fifteen Most Important Words

My dear friend, Lt. Col. Bruce Swezey, was a KC-135 pilot with the Wisconsin Air National Guard for many years and now is a captain for Midwest airlines, based in Milwaukee. Bruce is also a Bible scholar who fills my heart and head with the wonder of God's words. One day I asked Bruce, "What are the most important words you ever learned?"

I waited expectantly, anxious to hear something profound from the Bible that I could memorize and use on a daily basis.

"The most important words I ever learned?" Bruce repeated the question. A big smile broke out on his face and without blinking he said, "The thirty-nine-word bold print *Emergency Action for Spin Recovery*."

"The what?" I asked incredulously. *Emergency Action for Spin Recovery* didn't sound too Biblical to me.

Bruce took a breath, then rattled off the thirty-nine words in less than twelve seconds:

> "Throttles: idle. Rudder and ailerons: neutral. Stick: abruptly full aft and hold. Rudder: abruptly apply full rudder opposite spin direction, opposite turn needle, and hold. Stick: full forward one turn after applying rudder. Controls: neutral and recover from dive."

Bruce learned this life-saving method of getting an airplane out of a downward spin when he was in pilot's training after he graduated from the Air Force Academy in the 70s.

I laughed at his lightning fast performance and agreed that those thirty-nine words could certainly save Bruce's life and the lives of his passengers if, for some reason, his plane ever did get into a spin.

Then we began to talk about the words of the Bible. Were the most important words in the Old or New Testaments? Were the most powerful words written in Psalms or in Proverbs? How about the Ten Commandments? The Beatitudes? It was a fun discussion, but obviously one we did not finish or solve because it is impossible to decide which of God's words are the most important.

Later that day, when I was alone, I kept thinking, *What are the most important words I can say to my children, friends, coworkers?* For some reason, I wanted to find ten, fifteen, perhaps twenty important words. I wanted to memorize them.

I went to my collection of clever, interesting and inspirational sayings. I had a whole file folder full of them, collected since I was in college. I got it out and started reading.

One quote after another. Some from famous people, others not so famous. All interesting, thought-provoking, lively, some funny, others serious. But none of them had the impact that I was looking for. I wanted the most important words.

What did I want my most important words to accomplish? I asked myself. I thought about Bruce's recovery from a spin. I wanted my important words to help me recover from the spin I often found myself in as I tried to raise four children on my own. I wanted my important words to help me get more things accomplished in life. I wanted those words to help me find the answer to many problems. They should help me communicate my real feelings to others and to get along better with all sorts of people and help me show my appreciation for them. I wanted them also to help me maintain a positive attitude no matter how much of a spin I was in. I listed all of these demands on a piece of paper. And then I wrote down fifteen simple words that accomplished all that: *I love you. What is your opinion? I am proud of you. Thank you. Yes.*

Fifteen words. Five simple sentences. I decided to use my fifteen words every day, especially with my children. Amazing things happened. People around me started to beam with pride in their accomplishments. The children, especially, became more affectionate. Whenever I asked for someone's opinion I often received such creative solutions to problems that I was dumbfounded. I started writing more thank-you notes and saying yes more often to my friends when they asked for favors or when they asked if I wanted to join them for some adventure or another. Becoming a *yes* person means that when a new opportunity presents itself you automatically say *yes* and only say *no* if it's immoral, illegal or unhealthy. Believe me, the world loves an optimist. Haven't you ever noticed that yes people usually have more friends and more adventures than they know what to do with?

I've laminated my fifteen words and taped them next to my kitchen sink so I'm reminded many times a day to say those words as much as possible. Those fifteen words are my cornerstone for happiness, adventure, learning, contentment and appreciation.

Try it for a week. Believe in these words. *Say I love you, What is your opinion?, I am proud of you, Thank you* and *Yes,* more often yourself and see if your life and your happiness don't improve by giant leaps. Sometimes having *something to believe in* is simply a matter of learning to believe in simple acts of kindness.

Ground Zero

Three months after September 11, 2001, I found myself walking the perimeter of Ground Zero in lower Manhattan with four other women. My cousin Karen and I had flown from Wisconsin to New York to attend the opening of my daughter Jeanne's art show at a gallery in mid-Manhattan. Karen, a nurse, wanted to see Ground Zero because she hoped to return for three weeks as a Red Cross volunteer to help care for the police and firefighters who would be working there twenty-four hours a day for at least another year.

On that clear crisp December day, Jeanne, Karen and I invited my dear friend Mary Ann, a New Yorker by love and by choice, to join us. Mary Ann and I have been friends since 1982.

The fifth woman with us that Sunday was Ellen, who taught art with my daughter at Long Island University. Ellen lived in an apartment just blocks from the World Trade Center area and actually witnessed both planes crashing into the towers and the buildings imploding. Like hundreds of others she dialed 911 the moment it happened.

None of the five of us had been to Ground Zero before that day and somehow we knew it was something we needed to do as a group. We walked and walked around the perimeter, stared, wondered, shook our heads, shed tears and watched the firefighters still working, three months later, to put out the fires deep underground. We breathed in the acrid air that filtered up from below the streets and smelled like burning plastic. We saw hundreds of people filing by St. Paul's Chapel, where tall fences were installed to hold thousands of flowers, notes, letters, posters and the pouring out of love and grief from a nation of people who cannot comprehend what happened on those sixteen acres in New York City's oldest section.

We walked down the street where half-a-dozen huge dump trucks lined up to take their turn to remove the steel and the ashes of the dead. We five women understood that the air was filled with toxic chemicals and perhaps everyone should wear masks to protect themselves down there, but we didn't. Somehow it seemed that if we physically breathed it in, we would understand it better. Ellen mentioned that by breathing we became a part of the dead.

Ground Zero is a holy place. People are quiet, respectful. On one narrow street where we had to step over broken sidewalks and makeshift wooden walkways, there were a dozen handmade signs begging, "Please, no photographs or videos." But around the corner, down another street there were people taking snapshots and filming the hubbub in and around the gaping hole. The mind cannot comprehend such devastation, nor remember the details, so photos are necessary.

I wanted to remember the coarse, black, wet ashes in front of the church two blocks from where the towers stood. I wanted to remember the chain-link fences that protected the workers and the people who flocked to that neighborhood.

Most of all I need to remember how it felt to walk south a few blocks to Battery Park at the very tip of Manhattan where we could see the Statue of Liberty in the harbor. We five women stood on the dock where people board the ferry that takes them to the statue and then on to the immigration museum on Ellis Island. We arrived at the park just at sunset. The colors over the ocean screamed with red-orange brilliance as if all was well in New York.

There was a huge photographic mural covering a building at the dock with enormous images of Gandhi and Martin Luther King reminding visitors of lives dedicated to peace. To the left was the sunset, the statue of Lady Liberty, the ocean. To the right, a view of the skyscrapers of lower Manhattan, New Amsterdam, the oldest section of New York where the Trade Center for the world once stood. Only the skyline was missing its two most dramatic pieces. The gaping space between buildings was obscene, unfathomable, especially if you'd been to New York before and could remember exactly where the Towers stood. Sixteen acres of buildings, gone.

As we five women took in that sunset punctuated with the Statue of Liberty to the south and then looked north to where the giant towers once stood, each of us experienced muddled thoughts about the world and about our lives before and after September 11. To see that much death and destruction up close or to live and work near where America was attacked does something to your soul.

As we walked toward the subway my daughter put her arm around my waist. I reached for Mary Ann's hand. Karen and Ellen walked close together, sharing their feelings about life after 9/11.

We five women in our thirties, forties, fifties and sixties, together for one afternoon, represented a scattering of different relationships. But for three hours that day we were sisters united in faith who experienced awe, fear, anger, depression, amazement, loyalty, patriotism and the friendship that comes when people share their emotions. We saw a skyline that was different than before. But we also saw the Statue of Liberty and the sunset. We saw wet ashes and mangled steel on one side of a street and a sunset of enormous brilliance and beauty on the other. It was good to see them both together and to know that even though the skyline of New York will never be the same, the work and hope arising from the ashes in lower Manhattan is the stuff of liberty and sunrises and sunsets so beautiful you simply can't define them. You need to go there to understand how faith in action works. Sometimes *something to believe in* can only be experienced on a field trip.

Best Day Ever

We've all had one or more of those life-changing phone calls.

"Mom, I'm in the hospital."

"Mom, I'm pregnant!"

"Mom, I really need to borrow a thousand dollars right away."

Sometimes those phone calls stop your heart with anguish and fear. Sometimes they're downright joyous. Other times they make your head spin. I received a headspinner on a hot day in July 2002.

"Mom, Canyon and I have decided to get married . . . in three days. We want you to come!"

It was my oldest daughter, the one armed with a master's degree in fine art from Yale University, the one whose college loans surpass the entire annual budget for a medium size state. The one whose Jewish boyfriend our entire family rated a ten on the scale of great catches.

When you get one of those phone calls you suddenly feel like a trapeze artist for Ringling Brothers. Your heart does a few wild swings back and forth while you desperately wonder if this is going to be a regular wedding and if so how on earth are they going to pull it off in three days. Then your mind grabs the trapeze, does a giant flip and catches the bar at the last possible second when your daughter tells you it's going to be a simple civil ceremony at the court house, then a do-it-yourself spiritual event at a park afterwards, then lunch and a boat ride.

Ah, they've made all the plans, you think to yourself. You're off the hook. And it sounds like fun! Just go and enjoy.

"We were going to elope, but then a few of our friends found out and well, I think there will be about a dozen people now, including you."

This is the place where the mother begins to stammer and stutter, "Uh, well, where are you getting married exactly? Will there be a reception? Is it a dressy event? When should I come? You say it's this Thursday? I could be there day after tomorrow, Wednesday morning. Is that okay?"

As my heart continued the flip-flops, my mouth asked more inane questions. Jeanne finally interrupted. "Mom, we're getting married at City Hall in lower Manhattan, not too far from Ground Zero. Then we're going to Riverside Park next to the Hudson River to have a religious ceremony. Then we'll have a late lunch in an outdoor café near the river. And then we're all taking the Circle Line Harbor Lights sunset cruise around lower Manhattan."

"Sounds wonderful, my dear. See you Wednesday."

At that moment I thanked God for my daughter's common sense and her organizational skills. I also breathed a sigh of relief for my airline pilot friends who'd given me some inexpensive standby passes. I'd be flying to New York in two days. I especially thanked God that Jeanne, like me, had not inherited any big-wedding planning genes. Big weddings with their outlandish extravagances and megastress give me the heebie-jeebies. Imagine, a New York wedding and all I had to do was get there, try to be a little useful and enjoy the day.

The best things about Jeanne and Canyon's wedding? The pure, delicious unrehearsed fun of it all, for one thing. Watching Jeanne get dressed in the lovely, handmade, unpretentious, midnight blue, fitted street-length dress from the 1950s that she bought at a resale shop for fifteen dollars. Being asked by the bride and groom to make a *chuppah* (a Jewish wedding canopy) the morning of the wedding. Just give me a hot glue gun, lots of ribbon, an umbrella and I'm in cheaven. It was a grand chuppah.

What else did I love about that day? The three of us taking the New York subway to get to the court house and on our way to the subway, stopping in a small restaurant to ask the owner if we could have one of their starched white dinner napkins to wrap around the wine glass that Canyon planned to smash at the end of the ceremony in the park . . . and the startled

Middle-Eastern owner smiling, finally understanding our need, bowing, handing over the napkin as she said in broken English, "Congratulations, congratulations!"

It was a day of giggling absurdity at the very crabby magistrate and her forty-five-second civil ceremony; then profound spirituality as Canyon and Jeanne exchanged rings again and read prayers in the park in what seemed like much more of a wedding than the courthouse event. It was a day of light-hearted wonder, perfect weather and smuggled champagne onto the Circle Line tour boat.

It was commitment before God and state. A wedding, pure and simple. A day blessed with spontaneity, the laughter of friends, the deep love of husband and wife and the awe and joy of one very happy, very proud mother.

Best of all it was *something to believe in.* That two common-sense people can come together after mind-numbing events in their city the year before and cling to each other in a lifetime promise and make it work. When it's a wedding like that, everything you believe in suddenly becomes good and clean and pure and you just know, yes, you just know that this is *something to believe in* that is very, very good indeed.

Canceling the Pity Party

I wasn't looking forward to my fifty-seventh birthday. The angst I felt when I turned the milestone birthdays of thirty, forty and fifty was nothing compared to the dread of the fifty-seventh. Twenty-three years earlier, my mother had died at age fifty-seven of ALS—Lou Gehrig's disease. I could hardly believe mother was only fifty-seven when she died. I'm so young, I thought. *I had no* idea she was this young when she died.

How many more years do I have? I wondered.

As a single parent, my four children had been out on their own for years living in California, Arizona and two of them eighty and one hundred miles away in Wisconsin. I'd broken up with my last boyfriend ten years earlier so there was no man around to orchestrate my birthday. I did spend the first half of the day with my daughter Julia and her three youngsters, who had driven the hundred miles from their home in Dane, Wisconsin. This normally would have redeemed the day, but Julia was in the middle of an exhausting divorce and took a four-hour nap after lunch. Stress and tension seemed to ooze out of her pores and by the time they left I, too, was exhausted.

Alone again, I walked into my house and promptly began a grand pity party. Did I do anything constructive or fun to pull myself out of the doldrums? Of course not. The pity-party rules demand that you make yourself as miserable as possible.

No presents. No cake. The cards from my relatives and friends had all come in the mail a couple days earlier. My oldest daughter in California hadn't called. As in previous years, she thought my birthday was on the fourteenth instead of the twelfth of October.

My pity party continued, complete with tears and a bit of anger. Then I simply wished that those twenty-four hours would end quickly. I even started talking out loud to God, "Okay, God, I'm a nice, happy, fun, pleasant person. I have lots of friends, great kids, wonderful relatives. Some of them must remember that it's my birthday. So why am I alone tonight? I do stuff for other people on their birthdays. Is there something you want me to learn from this dismal experience?"

In a last-ditch effort to find something productive to do that evening, I gathered the trash and took it out to the garage. On my way back in to the house I spotted my bicycle in the corner. An old boyfriend had given it to me for Christmas twelve years earlier. I never really liked that bike. It didn't fit me right and the gears slipped like crazy in spite of a tune-up a few months earlier. I kicked the back tire and said, "You're about as worthless as I feel. I wish I had a new bike."

"That's it!" I practically shouted. "I'm going to buy myself a birthday present. A new bicycle! I'll go shopping for it tomorrow morning."

I'd been wanting a new bicycle for three years, but when a single mom is in her seventeenth year of having kids in college without a break, one does not think of extravagant purchases for oneself. But my black mood pushed me over the edge of self-indulgence.

Having made the decision, I practically skipped into the house, feeling thirty years younger and filled with the anticipation of a brand new bicycle. I was a kid again, dreaming of a sleek new lightweight aluminum-frame bike with shock absorbers and a comfortable seat.

That night, before bedtime, I was paging through the book of Psalms, trying to find a good definition of happiness. I found it in Psalm 144:12-15 (TLB).

Sons vigorous and tall as growing plants.
Daughters of graceful beauty like the pillars of a palace wall.
Barns full to the brim with crops of every kind.
Sheep by the thousands out in our fields.
Oxen loaded down with produce.
No enemy attacking the walls, but peace everywhere.
No crime in our streets.
Yes, happy are those whose God is Jehovah.

The verse described my sons, my daughters and my life perfectly. I thought to myself, *I'm healthy, have plenty to eat, no enemies attacking my walls, no crime in my streets and I have a wonderful friend in the Lord. This birthday is just another day. Most definitely, all is right in my world.*

Monday morning dawned and my new bicycle excitement hadn't waned a bit. I drove to the bike shop and rode a sleek silver and white lightweight aluminum-framed beauty around the store. I felt as excited as I was at age seven when I got my first bike fifty years earlier. This dream-bike was even on sale because it was the fall season. I pulled out my checkbook and paid in full.

Since then whenever I feel a little pity party coming on, or a lapse of faith as I sometimes call it, I hop on my twenty-one-speed beauty with the shock absorbers and a spring-loaded seat for extra comfort and head for the forty-nine-mile-long bike trail, which is just two miles from my new home in Florida. An hour later with another ten or twelve miles under my belt, my sunny disposition has returned. I've learned that when you're a big kid, every day can be a birthday celebration, an expression of faith. Especially when you have a good bicycle with a nice soft seat waiting to take you away.

Good health? Happiness? A great disposition? A positive attitude? It's all right there for the taking. I just have to understand that I alone am responsible for my own happiness. It's up to me to find ways to turn my pity party into a reason to be happy.

I believe it's possible. And I believe when I do that, then all the gusto that life holds is mine for the taking. In addition to basic faith, believing in my own power to change my own attitude, gives me lots more of *something to believe in.*

Of course, a brand new bicycle helps.

Salute to Singles

One thing I know. In order to be happy, I have to believe in myself and who I am at any given moment. Me? I'm single. I live alone. I love it. My very lifestyle gives me *something to believe in* every single day of my life. I know who I am, what it takes to make me happy, and what I had to do to get here. For me, being single is a choice that has worked for me for over two decades.

More than forty percent of all adults in the United States are single. Some never married, some divorced, some widowed. And like many people in this country I've lived a see-saw life between singlehood and marriage. First I was single. Then I was married. Then single. Then married again. Then single again. Three single periods in my life, thanks to two divorces. The first time, from birth to marriage, lasted twenty-three years. The second time I was single lasted almost three years. The third has lasted since 1985 and this time, I do believe, I'm starting to get the hang of it. Now that I know who I am, I can own my singleness. It's something to believe in, something that gives me power, independence, a sense of wellbeing and a reason to be proactive when it comes to friendships, travel, activities and just living life to the fullest.

I think about single people a lot and how many people in America don't honor the state of singlehood as much as we perhaps should. So let's get on the bandwagon.

Since we have May for Mother's Day and June for Father's Day and September for Grandparents' Day, perhaps we could have April for Singles Day. It would be a month for all those never married, divorced or widowed people to celebrate their lives. To rejoice in the many wonderful aspects of this single-file lifestyle.

Too many singles of all ages spend their single lives *in waiting*. They wait for that splendid day when they'll meet the man or woman of their dreams so they can tie the knot (again) and spend their days in hand-holding bliss. Singles Day could remind singles, especially those of us who have been married and divorced, that being single is a wonderful way to live a life. It's its own entity. It's a powerful *something to believe in* way of life. Being single is fun and that we, as individuals with lots to offer our families and friends, can and should live our lives with as much joy, gusto, fulfillment, passion and happiness as married couples.

If I were in charge of Singles Day, I would make greeting cards and posters proclaiming the fun, funny, tender and psychological reasons why it's great to be single.

My list would contain such things as these:

☛ You can sleep in the middle of the bed if you want.

☛ There's only one alarm clock in your bedroom to irritate you in the wee hours.

☛ Toothpaste is always rolled up the way you like.

☛ You don't have to pick up after another adult.

☛ Your favorite healthy cereal doesn't disappear after two days.

☛ You can spend time with your friends any time you want for as long as you want.

☛ You get to make all the decisions without long discussions or arguments.

☛ You never have to drive around for hours with someone who refuses to ask for directions.

☛ You don't have to feel guilty for being in control of the checkbook.

☛ The car seat is always in the right position.

☛ You get to be head of household without any arguments.

☛ There's nobody at home telling you what to do, how to do it, when it do it, or how much money you can spend doing it.

☛ You can cook what you want when you want including having popcorn for lunch or eating your dessert first.

☛ You can cook twice a week and eat leftovers the rest of the time.

☛ You can go out to eat every night if you've had it with cooking.

☛ You can rearrange the furniture any way you want as often as you want.

☛ You can tear whatever you want out of the newspaper, even if you're the first person to read it.

☛ Your friends can drop into your home anytime without an invitation and nobody's going to get upset.

☛ You never have to wait for your spouse to get out of the bathroom so you can get ready.

☛ You can clean house as much or as little as you want.

☛ No one will keep reminding you that you've put on a few pounds since last year.

☛ You never have to balance your checkbook if you don't want to.

☛ No one is going to throw a fit if you put a little dent in the car.

☛ You can eat cookies in bed and listen to the radio at 3:00 AM without bothering anybody.

If I was going to make greeting cards for folks to give to single people on Singles Day, I'd have pictures of happy singles swimming, inline skating, hiking, biking, riding hot-air balloons or just walking down the sidewalk alone, enjoying life. I'd show pictures of restaurants with table settings made up for one or three, not, as always, two or four.

If I was going to write a prayer for single people on Singles Day, I'd say something like *Heavenly Father, be with my single friends and me as we live our single-file life in a two-by-two world. Help us to cherish our freedom and to use our energy to befriend and find joy in being with other singles.*

If I was going to think up gift ideas for Singles Day, I'd suggest gift certificates from handymen, seamstresses, great cooks, housecleaners and car mechanics.

Here's to the 40.3% of all the adults in America who are single. May we all be as happy, fulfilled and whole as our married friends as we march through life single file, one by one. May we believe in and cherish our lifestyle. I just think it's important to believe in who you are at any given time of your life, married, single, divorced, widowed, separated. *Something to believe in?* Believe in you.

Bicycle Prayers

I admit it. In church, I watch, sing, daydream and on a good day, say a few perfunctory prayers, only because everybody else is saying them out loud as well. But often my heart and the depth of my soul are not in the church experience. I'm too distracted by the people in front of me, behind me, next to me, and especially the squirmy preschoolers within a ten-foot range.

As long as I'm confessing it all right here, I might as well admit another sorry truth. I rarely listen to sermons in church. Too much "telling" and not enough "showing" I suppose. I must be a slow learner. I need concrete examples if I'm going to get the message. I want the pastor to tell me a story about the time he mouthed off to his mother, for instance, and how he learned to respect and treat her with kindness because of such an interesting incident. I don't want to hear the fire and brimstone of gas being poured over the charcoal briquettes of eternal damnation if I don't do as I'm told. And even if the message is mild-mannered, it's the heavy theology that causes my brain to take a vacation.

My not being prayerful enough and not paying close attention in church used to fill me with gut-wrenching guilt but that ended one fine day in Largo, Florida, on a bike trail that winds gracefully through one of the most beautiful parks I've ever seen. It was the end of November and my friends back home in Wisconsin were shoveling snow in single-digit temperatures. I was on a bicycle in seventy-five-degree sunshine soaking up such pure joy I was about to burst.

I started praying like I'd never prayed before. I felt like Adam and Eve in paradise. Zigging and zagging on that meandering bike trail amidst tall evergreens, mighty oaks, flowering bushes, an occasional crane, heron or egret punctuating the large lake like lawn ornaments back home. Prayers spilled out of my heart like letters falling out of a Scrabble bag.

Instead of just rattling off my long list of "Please, God, do this and that for me," it was a litany of praising and glorifying God for the beautiful landscape. I thanked him for my absolute, pure, unabated happiness. I moved on to asking God for forgiveness for all my transgressions, impatience, insensitive behavior, selfishness and speaking before I think sometimes. Next, I forgave my trespassers and then petitioned the Almighty for favors for others.

Being on my bike in the warm sunshine in a beautiful place lifted the cobwebs that fill the corners of my psyche. I can't help myself. I simply have to pray when I'm on my bicycle.

I saw Spanish moss hanging from huge southern oak trees and I thanked God for every thing green and growing, including the seven-foot alligator sunning himself on a tiny island in the lake a few feet from the bike trail. When I crossed the street into the Botanical Garden area I stopped in the rose garden to smell every single one of the ten or so varieties of roses in bloom and then continued on the bike path praising and thanking God for flowers.

Each day as I extended my solitary bike rides from seven miles to fifteen miles, then one day I even went twenty-seven miles, my prayers grew in depth, intensity and number. I asked God to help me sort out problems. I prayed for answers to dilemmas facing my children. The answers sometimes surprised me, but there were answers nonetheless. As the miles clicked by on the odometer, the prayers multiplied in number.

When I began my bicycling career in Wisconsin, God provided a place of grace and prayer for my bike rides. Just two blocks from my home (this is before I moved to Florida permanently, mind you) there was an exquisite, wide, asphalted bike trail that meandered hither and yon for dozens and dozens of miles. In the warm weather months I'd hop on my bike and pray, sing and even meditate while pedaling. The giant thank-you's to God for my good health and that bike trail reached a glorifying pitch when I came upon my favorite place where the bike trail winds breathtakingly along the shore of Lake Michigan.

Sometimes in the woods I'd see deer, usually a mother and two fawns. That's when I thanked God for all the animals, tame and wild. Berry bushes, maple trees on fire with color in the fall and the occasional foot bridge over the Oak Creek that swayed back and forth in my old neighborhood also brought out the best prayers my bike rides have to offer.

So there it is, my entire confession. I'm not the best prayer person in church, but I'm a prayerful whizbang on my bicycle with the wind blowing through my hair and God's amazing creations before me. *Something to believe in.* This amazing, glorious world. What a gift!

Some Have It All

Every once in a great while you meet someone who seems to have it all together. Usually it's an older person who has lived life, experienced life's struggles and has grown and matured because of those struggles. They've figured it all out. They know what it takes to be happy in this world. *Something to believe in.* And because they have that belief, they have become wise.

Rarely does a younger person have it figured out. But Jacob was such a person. In addition to having lots of *someones to love* in his life, he had *something to do*, boy, did he ever! He had *something to hope for.* And he had plenty of laughter. But most importantly, he had *something to believe in* . . . megatheories, philosophies, a code of ethics and behavior and faith-based spirituality.

As a very little boy Jacob figured out that *something to do* was an important part of the happiness equation. Not only that, he learned firsthand that when you do something for others, it truly makes you happier than if you're just doing something for yourself.

In grade school Jacob joined Cub Scouts and got his first taste of what organizations are all about. Later, at the large Catholic church his family attended, Jacob was an altar server for five years, helping the priest before, during and after the weekend masses.

For seven years, sixth grade through twelfth, he was an active member of the Orland Township Youth Commission in his town of Orland Park, Illinois, volunteering for numerous activities in that organization. Imagine, a kid that age, sticking with a volunteer organization for seven years.

In junior high he participated in and did volunteer work for the *Snowflake* drug awareness program. He continued as a volunteer in drug awareness in high school where the same organization was called *Snowball.*

When Jacob was a teenager he helped coach little kids at basketball and soccer camps. He helped demonstrate techniques and even did a little one-on-one coaching if some of the kids needed extra work.

He also worked with youngsters at summer day camps for children with behavioral issues. He helped walk the youngsters through trust-building exercises, team building and organized sports activities. He wasn't exactly a camp counselor there, but as a teenage volunteer he was able to be lots more than a babysitter for the children at camp.

At holiday parties at the various youth organizations that Jacob participated in when he was a young teenager, he helped organize the party supplies, loaded trucks and went out of his way to make the kids feel welcome, even told a few jokes.

When his community in the suburb southwest of Chicago held community-wide 5K (five kilometer) walks or runs, Jacob was the first to sign up to hand out water to participants and cheer them on.

In high school Jacob was a participant in the cancer walk events—he got pledges, then did the overnight walks to help raise funds for the organization.

There were two leadership groups at the high school that Jacob participated in—Senior Leaders and First Class. Senior Leaders helped the gym teachers run activities and coach the lower grades. First Class was a group of kids who helped educate the rest of the student body, often by performing skits that were aimed primarily at personal responsibility and behavior.

And finally, in high school, Jacob joined the Civil Air Patrol. Over the years he directed traffic at local fly-in events. He became the cadet leader of his squadron's search-and-rescue team, which would help locate planes whose ELT (Emergency Locator Transmitter) had gone off and been picked up by satellite. He would get calls in the middle of the night and had to leave at a moment's notice—so he always had a huge backpack in his room loaded with all the emergency gear he might need, including flashlights. Jacob loved flashlights . . . every color, size, style and function . . . always looking to light the way for others. During those search-and-rescue missions Jacob was credited with finding a number of planes, mostly either false alarms or planes with mechanical problems.

Jacob also worked on the flight line at the Experimental Aircraft Association airshow in Oshkosh, Wisconsin, in 2004, 2005 and 2006. He and his fellow cadets stood out by the runway and guided incoming aircraft to their designated areas.

A few times, as a CAP volunteer, Jacob and the other cadets would help tether hot air balloons at a local balloon show.

For several years Jacob volunteered at the Chicago Air and Water show, handing out programs to the crowd of over one million people.

During his years in the Civil Air Patrol Jacob learned of a young boy in sixth grade from his neighborhood who had also joined the Civil Air Patrol, but had no transportation. The youngster's mother, a single parent, worked long hours and couldn't get home in time to get her son to the meetings. So Jacob drove out of his way to pick up the sixth grader and took him to the meetings during Jacob's entire senior year of high school. Most teens aren't too crazy about having younger kids hanging around them, but Jacob didn't mind, and, in fact, treated the youngster like a little brother.

From the time he was a small child Jacob had flying in his blood. His uncle Joe, a 747 Captain for UPS, has been piloting planes for over thirty years. Jacob's grandfather, Ed Kobbeman, was a fighter pilot in World War II and even in his eighties was still doing take-off's and landings and flying around the countryside with his son Joe in a small plane. Both Jacob's uncle and his grandfather talked frequently to Jacob about flying. Joe even took him on a few trips in his own small plane and, of course, let Jacob do all the flying. Joe always said Jacob was a natural pilot and that his parents should let him take flying lessons.

In high school Jacob worked very hard to get his private pilot's license. When he was just sixteen years old he soloed, and fifteen months later, at age seventeen he passed all his tests, including his final check ride, and received his official license to be a pilot.

After that, every chance he got, he'd rent a small plane to build up his flying time, accumulating more than one hundred hours total. Jacob's love of flying seemed to be as important as breathing to him, so it's no wonder that long before he left for college he knew exactly what his major would be. Aviation, without a doubt.

And so it was that when Jacob was eighteen years old, like most bright young students, he left for college, heading north to the University of North Dakota, which boasts one of the best aviation schools in the country. But before he left, and because he'd been the commander of his Civil Air Patrol unit his last year in high school, Jacob decided to write a letter to Colleen, the young woman who was one of his closest friends and who took over his command when he left.

Colleen,

Becoming the cadet commander is a big step and will bring many new challenges and hard times. However, it will also bring the greatest rewards. I think that the key to success is to set goals and to never, ever give up on them. If there is only one thing that you remember from me, I want that last sentence to be it. That goes for being a cadet commander, but also in life in general. Don't ever give up on your dreams, no matter how impossible they seem.

During your term, just remember to use your staff to its fullest potential and always use other people to help come up with new ideas. Make sure that everyone respects you. I'm not talking about the kind of respect that is forced, but the kind that is earned. Make your people trust you and buy into your goals and dreams, once this is accomplished, you will be home free. I should say that this is no easy task; I for one have never been able to fully accomplish this.

You can skate through your term, not do much and get replaced in six months (like so many commanders before you have done), or you can try your best to make the squadron into the best it possibly can be. If you truly want it and will not give up until you get it, then you will be successful. The items on this CD are designed to help you be successful, so I hope you can sort through the junk and find something useful.

> Through the past three or so years, I've been able to get to know you rather well. We've had our ups and downs, but I think we have pretty much stabilized our friendship. I think that friendships like ours tend to last for decades, so I can only hope that is the case. I wish you the best of luck in your next few years, but also I would like to add a warning. I don't want to sound like your parents, but I truly care about you. You are very smart (both street and book, which is rather unusual), very pretty and very friendly. You have an amazingly bright future, and I could not stand to see something happen to you. Some things to watch out for are . . .
>
> Booze—If you get caught drinking under twenty-one, that could easily ruin your career, your dreams and your life. Maybe it's because I'm a pilot and that one thing would definitely put me on the streets, but I take that pretty seriously. So I personally don't think it's worth it. Plus it tastes gross, and makes you do stupid things, which brings me to my next thing to watch out for . . .
>
> Guys—News flash, at least seventy-five percent of the guys who will hit on you in college are just looking for some action. Be especially careful if you mix guys and booze, because if you pass out . . . God only knows what could happen.
>
> Uh . . . I guess that's all I really have for you right now, but I expect to have some sort of communication with you (e-mail, AIM, phone, etc.) at least once a week while I'm at college. So stay in touch.
>
> Much love,
>
> Jake

When I was eighteen years old, writing a letter like that would have been as foreign to me as discovering the theory of relativity. But not for Jacob. He was wise beyond his years with more common sense than most adults, let alone teenagers. He had so much to believe in.

When he arrived on campus, Jacob made friends with all the other aviation students. One friend, Jake Sundblad, and Jacob both joined the Army's ROTC program at the University of North Dakota's Fighting Sioux Battalion. ROTC was a huge part of their lives during that first semester of college. I mean really, how many college kids are willing to get up at 5:30 AM three times a week for rigorous physical training in order to follow their dreams? But they did it, week after week, for three months.

Sometimes, after classes, Jacob would rent a small plane and go flying to build up his hours. One cold night, December 1, 2006, just three months after starting their freshman year in college, Jacob, age eighteen, and his friend Jake, nineteen, rented a small two-passenger plane, as they had done before to build up more hours. Jacob was at the controls and he took off in weather that may have been a bit marginal, but certainly good enough for a safe take-off. But something drastic happened just minutes after take-off, a squall moved in, the ceiling dropped to two hundred feet and the plane crashed, killing both young men instantly.

Jacob was my only sister's only son and as Jacob's Aunt Pat, I am witness to the fact that he lived a life packed with richness in so many ways that few of us ever achieve even into our sixties, seventies or eighties.

That young man had a maturity about him that spoke loud and clear to me. He had it all . . . all five ingredients to happiness:

Someone to love

All of us in his entire large family felt his love as did his friends, colleagues and teachers.

Something to do

Wow, did he ever have plenty to do! Flying, college, friends, family, volunteer activities.

Something to hope for

Jacob's hopes included getting his college degree, having a career as a pilot and continuing giving to his community and to his country. He hoped that someday he might even fly helicopters for the U.S. military.

Something to believe in

Jacob's faith led him to give to others in so many ways from the time he was a little boy. His belief system was the core of him that seemed to be lodged along his spine, making him stand ramrod straight in his principles and in the way he carried himself as a young man on the cusp of life.

Something to Laugh About

How many times did his littleboy laughter delight us when he beat us at a rousing family game of Tripoly or Poker? How many giggles did he share and instigate with his goofy practical jokes with friends, family, coworkers and fellow students? So many we can't even count.

No doubt about it, Jacob had it all. He was one of the happiest kids I ever knew. And why not? He possessed all five of the essential ingredients for happiness.

In life, Jacob would have been a hero. In death, he is an inspiration and a guardian angel to everyone who knew and loved him. For our family, at least, Jacob's life and death give us the promise of life eternal. *Something to believe in.* When you've known someone like Jacob you just know there's more to this place than meets the eye. There simply has to be.

Madeline L'Engle once asked, "Why does anybody tell a story?" She went on to answer the question, "It does indeed have something to do with faith," she said, "faith that the universe has meaning, that our little human lives are not irrelevant, that what we choose or say or do matters, matters cosmically."

Jacob matters cosmically. All people do. I'm happy because I have faith that his death, their deaths and lives, have meaning. I may not understand it all exactly just yet, but having *something to believe in* and knowing that Jacob did too, just makes it easier to smile, be happy and know that someday after I die, then I'll understand.

Chapter Six

Something to Laugh About

You don't stop laughing because you grow old,
you grow old because you stop laughing.
—*Author unknown*

I'm a big fan of laughter. The gift of laughter is such an important ingredient for happiness that I've saved it for last. It's the one ingredient that turns happiness into joy, into giggles, into slap-your-thigh outrageous wonderment and delight at life itself. Laughter is happiness turned vocal.

Laughter is in my main-ingredients-for-happiness list because it is a critical part of our physical and mental well-being. Joy from our inner souls spills out from our bodies as laughter. Laughter releases endorphins, which also help build up the immune system that keeps us healthy by fighting off sickness, germs, viruses, infections and disease. Laughter massages our internal organs and increases oxygen to the blood by ten times, thus raising our energy levels.

Laughter reduces our blood pressure. One minute of hearty laughter can produce a heart rate equal to that of ten minutes of rowing on an exercise machine. Laughter benefits the respiratory tract, helping people at risk for pulmonary infection to clear their lungs of air containing carbon dioxide and water vapor and replace it with oxygen-rich air. Coughing produced by laughter can clear the trachea and bronchi of mucus. Laughter makes you breathe from a deeper place in the lungs. It relaxes the skeletal muscles in the arms and legs to improve circulation. Watching a funny movie can eliminate tension and anger and greatly ease depression.

Laughter also helps us mentally. It improves our moods, reduces depression, helps us sleep and it brings us into the present where there is love and hope, not in the past where there may be sadness or regret.

Career counselors and human resource people look for people with a good sense of humor because studies have shown that such people have better problem-solving skills and are usually more creative than people who don't have a sense of humor.

On my desk in my writing room, next to my computer where I can see it at all times, is a picture of Jesus laughing. His eyes are sparkling, cheeks rosy, mouth wide open, head back. It just makes me happy to look at that painting. Granted, Jesus didn't sit still for the portrait, but I think whoever painted it had a pretty accurate idea of Jesus' personality. Jesus and the painter both knew the importance of laughter.

Luckily laughter has seeped into my life often and long. My dad has a great sense of humor and taught all three of his kids how to instigate, appreciate and detonate laughter.

In December 1997, my dad, who was seventy-eight years old at the time, sent me a handwritten letter on holiday paper. He wrote, *Dear Pat, Since you will be leaving in a few days I have placed your name at the top of my drudgery list. Already I can feel the tension building. My usual sunny disposition is waning, my face is flushed and my feet seemed swollen when putting on my socks and shoes. The next thing will be total constipation, and all because I have to write forty Christmas letters.*

Dad often resorts to humor when stress gets the best of him. Works every time, too, because ten years later, at age eighty-eight, he's still writing Christmas letters. Not as many though, because many of his friends have sailed on to the next life.

One of my all-time great jokes, and certainly my favorite that I ever played on anyone was the one I played on my mother for seventeen years. During that time neither of us ever talked about the joke or laughed about it with each other. However, during those years of the baggy yellow shirt joke, I laughed more with other people about the joke than you can imagine. I'm sure my happiness quotient soared each time I hid the shirt at mother's house and each time I found it hidden in mine. Here's the story from the beginning.

The Baggy Yellow Shirt

The baggy yellow shirt had long sleeves, four extra-large pockets trimmed in black thread and snaps up the front. Not terribly attractive, but utilitarian without a doubt. I found it in December 1963, during my freshman year in college when I was back home in Illinois on Christmas break.

Part of the fun of every vacation at home was the chance to go through Mom's hoard of rummage, destined for the less fortunate. She regularly scoured the house for clothes, bedding and housewares to give away, storing them in brown paper bags on the floor of the front hall closet.

Looking through Mom's collection one day, I came across an oversized yellow shirt, slightly faded from years of wear but still in decent shape.

"Just the thing to wear over my clothes during art class," I said to myself.

"You're not taking that old thing, are you?" Mom asked when she saw me packing it. "I wore that when I was pregnant with your brother in 1954!"

"It's perfect for art class, Mom. Thanks." I slipped it into my suitcase before she could object.

The baggy yellow shirt became a part of my college wardrobe. I loved it. All during college, it stayed with me, always comfortable to throw on over my clothes during messy projects. The underarm seams had to be reinforced before I graduated, but there was plenty of wear left in that old shirt.

After graduation I moved to Denver and wore the shirt the day I moved into my new apartment. Then I wore it on Saturday mornings when I cleaned. Those four large pockets on the front—two breast pockets and two at hip level—made a super place to carry dust cloths, wax and spray cleaner.

The next year, I married. When I became pregnant, I found the yellow shirt tucked in a drawer and wore it during those big-belly days. Though I missed sharing my first pregnancy with Mom and Dad and the rest of my family, since we were in Colorado and they were in Illinois, that shirt helped remind me of their warmth and protection. I smiled and hugged the shirt when I remembered that Mother had worn it when she was pregnant.

By 1969 when my daughter was born, that shirt was at least fifteen years old. That Christmas, I patched one elbow, washed and pressed the shirt, wrapped it in holiday paper and sent it to Mom. Smiling, I tucked a note in one of the pockets saying: "I hope this fits. I'm sure it will look great on you!" When Mom wrote to thank me for her "real" gifts, she said the yellow shirt was lovely. Neither Mother nor I ever mentioned it again.

The next year, my husband, daughter and I moved from Denver to St. Louis. We stopped at Mom and Dad's house in Rock Falls, Illinois, to pick up some furniture they were giving us. Days later, when we uncrated the old kitchen table that had belonged to my grandmother, I noticed something yellow taped to its bottom. The baggy yellow shirt! And so the pattern was set.

On our next visit home, I secretly placed the shirt between the mattress and box springs of Mom and Dad's bed. I don't know how long it took her to find it, but almost two years passed before I got it back.

By then our family had grown—another daughter, then a year later a son.

This time Mom got even with me. She put the yellow shirt under the base of our living-room lamp, knowing that as a mother of three little ones, housecleaning and moving floor lamps would not be everyday events for me.

When I finally found the shirt, I wore it often while refinishing "early marriage" furniture that I found at rummage sales. The walnut stains on the shirt simply added more character to its history.

Unfortunately, our lives were full of stains too.

My marriage had been failing almost from the beginning. After a number of attempts at marriage counseling, my husband and I divorced in 1975. The three children and I prepared to move back to Illinois to be closer to the emotional support of family and friends.

As I packed, a deep depression overtook me. I wondered if I could make it on my own with three small children to raise. I wondered if I would find a job. One night I paged through my Bible looking for comfort. In Ephesians, I read, "So use every piece of God's armor to resist the enemy whenever he attacks, and when it is all over, you will be standing up."

I tried to picture myself wearing God's armor, but all I saw was me wearing the stained yellow shirt. Of course! Wasn't my mother's love a piece of God's armor? I smiled and remembered the fun and warm feeling the yellow shirt had brought into my life over the years. My courage was renewed and somehow the future didn't seem so alarming.

Unpacking in our new home and feeling much better, I knew I had to get the shirt back to Mother. The next time I visited her, I carefully tucked it in her bottom dresser drawer where she kept her winter sweaters, knowing that sweater weather was months away.

Meanwhile my life moved splendidly. I found a good job at a radio station and the children thrived in their new environment.

A year later during a window-washing spurt, I found the crumpled yellow shirt hidden in a rag bag in my cleaning closet. Something new had been added. Emblazoned across the top of the breast pocket were the bright green newly embroidered words, *I BELONG TO PAT.* Not to be outdone, I got out my own embroidery materials and added an apostrophe and seven more letters. Now the shirt proudly proclaimed, *I BELONG TO PAT'S MOTHER.*

Once again, I zigzagged all the frayed seams. Then I enlisted the aid of a dear friend, Harold, to help me get it back to Mom. He arranged to have a friend mail the shirt to Mom from Arlington, Virginia. We enclosed a letter announcing that she was the recipient of an award for her good deeds. The award letter, on official looking stationery printed at the high school where Harold was assistant principal, came from "The Institute for the Destitute."

This was my finest hour. I would have given anything to see Mom's face when she opened the "award" box and saw the shirt inside. But, of course, she never mentioned it.

On Easter Sunday the following year, Mother managed the coup de grace. She walked into our home with regal poise, wearing that old shirt over her Easter outfit, as if it were an integral part of her wardrobe.

I'm sure my mouth hung open, but I said nothing. During the Easter meal, a giant laugh choked my throat. But I was determined not to break the unbroken spell the shirt had woven into our lives. I was sure that Mom would take off the shirt and try to hide it in my home, but when she and Dad left, she walked out the door wearing, *I BELONG TO PAT'S MOTHER* like a coat of arms.

A year later, in June 1978, Harold and I were married. The day of our wedding, we hid our car in a friend's garage to avoid the usual practical jokers. After the wedding, late that night while my husband drove us to our honeymoon suite in Wisconsin, I reached for a pillow in the backseat so I could rest my head. The pillow felt lumpy. I unzipped the case and discovered a gift, wrapped in wedding paper.

I thought it might be a surprise gift from Harold. But he looked as stunned as I. Inside the box was the freshly pressed baggy yellow shirt.

Mother knew I'd need the shirt as a reminder that a sense of humor, spiced with love, is one of the most important ingredients in a happy marriage. In a pocket was a note: "Read John 14:27–29. I love you both, Mother."

That night I paged through a Bible I found in the hotel room and found the verses: "I am leaving you with a gift—peace of mind and heart! And the peace I give isn't fragile like the peace the world gives. So don't be troubled or afraid. Remember what I told you: I am going away, but I will come back to you again. If you really love me, you will be very happy for me, for now I can go to the Father, who is greater than I am. I have told you these things before they happen so that when they do, you will believe in me." (TLB)

The yellow shirt was Mother's final gift.

She had known for three months before my wedding that she had a terminal disease, amyotrophic lateral sclerosis (Lou Gehrig's disease). Mother died thirteen months later, at age fifty-seven. I must admit that I was tempted to send the yellow shirt with her to her grave. But I'm glad I didn't, because it is a vivid reminder of the love-filled game she and I played for more than sixteen years.

Besides, my oldest daughter is in college now, majoring in art... and every student needs a baggy yellow shirt with big pockets to wear to art class.

Clothes Closet Capers

My fun with clothes didn't stop with the baggy yellow shirt. No, it continued on, and reached a peak, thanks to the fact that my daughters, Jeanne and Julia, had suddenly blossomed into teenagers. Teenagers who liked to shop.

Teenage daughters and mothers know what it's like. Shopping for clothes together at the local mall is a test of patience, physical endurance, restraint and basic human kindness. I remember many trips to the mall with my two daughters.

"Mother, give it up! These pants are way too baggy!"

"Honey, they're skin tight. They'd split if you sat down! And after they've been in the dryer, why . . ."

"Mom, you're so old-fashioned!"

Later, in the shoe store the sharp-edged conversation would begin again. "Well, Mom, these shoes are okay, I guess. They look just like the name-brand ones and they fit okay, but Mother, they don't have the right label. And that's why they're not cool. Everybody will know I got them at a discount store! I'll pay the twenty dollar difference myself for the name-brand ones, okay?"

"When donkeys fly, you will. If you have that kind of money to throw around, you can put it in your college fund."

We move on to the fancy dress store. "No Mom, I don't like that dress. It's straight out of the eighties! Do you actually think I'd be caught dead in a dress like that?"

"No, I was thinking more in terms of the homecoming dance, but if you keep talking to me like this. . . ."

Please, Lord, give me patience. Direct me out of this store and over to the place where they sell warm chocolate chip cookies. Quickly, Lord.

By the time they were in senior high I'd had about all the dismal, distressing, argumentative shopping trips I could stand. I decided to let them shop alone from then on with money they earned themselves.

Thanks, Lord, for that brilliant idea. Maybe I'll survive motherhood after all.

Then one day, a year or so later, it happened.

"Mom," Julia asked sweetly, "may I borrow your yellow blouse to wear to school tomorrow? And maybe your blue and yellow print skirt?"

"Sure, honey!" I practically fell off the stool at the kitchen counter. At last my daughters were growing up. Our taste in clothes was starting to meld. I suddenly felt ten years younger.

A few minutes later, Jeanne passed through the kitchen.

"Mom, could I try on some of your clothes? I might like to borrow your plaid skirt and one of your scarves."

"Help yourself, my dear," I smiled smugly as I turned up the music on their favorite radio station. *I love having daughters,* I thought to myself.

Oh, Lord, thank You. Either I'm getting really hip when it comes to clothes or they've finally discovered sensible fashion. Whatever it is, Lord, let me cherish this moment.

Suddenly, being a single mom was fun. Instead of fighting over the cost of clothes and the styles my daughters wanted versus those that actually made sense to me, visions of exciting mother-daughter shopping sprees danced in my head. *Why, now we can plan whole days of shopping,* I mused. *We'll look, share ideas about fashion and help each other choose styles that flatter us.* I continued to dream. *We'll have lunch together, quiche and croissants, iced tea . . . and maybe we three will split something for dessert, all the while discussing our bargains and look-alike fashions.* The dream was filling my heart with the joy of motherhood.

Just then Jeanne and Julia emerged from my bedroom dressed practically head-to-toe in fashions from my wardrobe, including jewelry and other accessories.

"Thanks, Mom! Your clothes are great!" they bubbled.

I wasn't so sure about the combinations they'd chosen, but I certainly wasn't about to criticize. After all, I didn't want to ruin this special moment . . . this tender passage from teendom to a more sophisticated world of young women.

"Yeah, they're perfect, Mom," Jeanne nodded. "It's nerd day at school tomorrow . . . you know, everybody dresses up like the fifties, real dorky-like. These things are perfect!"

"Oh . . ."

Lord, are You there? I need more patience, Lord. Lots more. Right this minute, Lord. Are You listening?

Oh yeah, I laughed about it later. Much later. In fact, that incident happened in the mideighties and as your children age, you tend to find things like that funnier by the minute.

Laughter, even when it's at your own expense, is definitely a happiness-maker.

Promises, Promises

Sometimes laughter comes at us in the form of the ridiculous. I know the little incident that follows caused me quite a few belly laughs.

One day I picked up a copy of one of those women's magazines that specializes in grueling, heart-wrenching chaos. Story after story of tragedy, divorce, infidelity, child and spouse abuse, loneliness, deception and heartbreak. It was a regular true-life soap opera that unfortunately smacks of home for many.

But after ten minutes of reading all about other people's miseries I flipped past the pages of trauma and tribulation and started reading the advertisements instead. (I can just hear the sponsors and their advertising companies cheering in the background right about now.) Those ads sparkled with good news, glowed with promise and filled my heart with expectations of a new me. The ads in that magazine offered a panacea of positiveness, the fountain of youth, hope and eternal beauty all rolled into a few how-did-I-ever-live-without-them products.

There I was, in my late forties and feeling rather glum about my excess baggage, crows' feet, gray hairs, double chin and gone-with-the-wind figure. My figure had gone from Scarlet to Mammy in less than a decade.

But hark. A new lease on life was waiting for me between the pages of that magazine.

I looked in the mirror and took a rather bleak inventory. What did I see? Thin, scraggly, medium-length hair with no body, a leftover dead-end perm with sun-bleached ends and lots of graybrown poking through the scalp. Surely this magazine, this glorious mecca of beauty, could do something about my disastrous locks.

As I scanned those pages, hope sprang forth. *Miracle lotion gives you stronger, thicker, longer hair in just five to seven days!*

Did that mean in a month I'd have luscious, rich, thick curls down my back? A full head of wavy hair like those television models who talk you into buying shampoo? What a scientific breakthrough!

The next ad was a real eye-catcher for me, a woman who has not been happy with her weight since fifth grade. *Super-crash-loss diet turns ugly fat into harmless water and flows it right out of your system by the gallon. Works so fast, you shrink down your waistline as much as a full size smaller in just twenty-four hours and four sizes smaller in just fourteen days.*

My devious mind said, *Ah, it's probably just a diuretic, a water pill.* But then I remembered the truth-in-advertising law. They'd have to tell you the truth if all it was was a water pill, right? I could hardly wait to start my super-crash-loss diet. The thought of turning all my ugly fat into harmless water was more exciting than a balloon ride with Mel Gibson or Tom Hanks. (Or both.)

I kept flitting from advertisement to advertisement. I was turning into a ravishing starlet before my eyes. The next ad sent chills up my back. *Bumps and bulges gone forever. No diet pills, no crash diets, no strenuous exercises.* My heart started to thump right through my faded blue oversize sweatshirt.

Bumps and bulges? My body has more bumps and bulges and

ups and downs than a rollercoaster at Great America. Now at last, I could rid myself of this plague, this joke of Mother Nature's, with no diet, no pills and no exercise.

How many years had I longed for a beautiful body without having to watch my diet or exercise? And all the time the secrets were hidden right here in this magazine, available to every man, woman and child in the good ole USA.

I knew it was time to fix supper for the family and time to throw another load in the washer. But I couldn't put down that magazine. I tried, but the words, *soothes away wrinkles*, jumped right off the page and I was hooked worse than before.

New wrinkle-removing formula. Instantly takes ten to fifteen years off your face. Gives you a satin smooth, petal soft, youthful complexion that lasts. Fifteen years off my face? What if I used it twice? Would it remove thirty years off my face? Why, I'd be nineteen again! No more laugh lines, crows' feet or road-map forehead.

The next page was even better. *Grow fresher, younger-looking skin while you sleep! Actually wake up looking ten, fifteen, twenty years younger just twenty-one mornings from now, or even sooner!*

Twenty years younger? Two doses of that brand and I'd look nine years old, younger than my own children. Yes! Where do I send my money?

And then, the hope of mothers everywhere, the dream of all dreams. *Stretch marks disappear instantly on hips, stomach, buttocks, breasts.* After delivering into this world four children, two of them ten and nine pounds respectively, I have stretch marks that look as if they were placed there with a branding iron. My abdomen has a road map of Pasadena deeply etched in fourteen karat stretch. Could it be true? Could I really wear hip-huggers? A bikini? Short shorts?

I read on. I daydreamed of the new me. I wondered how long it would take my orders to arrive and if I should have a *coming out* party with my new hair, waistline, breasts, body, face and abdomen. What would the kids think when they discovered I'd squandered the entire grocery budget for two months on the new me? Could I find sixty ways to fix beans and weenies? Would our happy little single parent home become a hodgepodge of activity as Mom had date after date with one gorgeous hunk of a man after another? Would my teenage daughters be jealous? Would the children enjoy having their friends ask if I was their sister? Would my friends be so insanely jealous that they'd never take me bowling again?

The promises loomed, page after page.

Remove unwanted hair forever.
Whiter, brighter teeth instantly.
Melt off inches in minutes.
Face-lift in a jar.

It was a marvelous hour. The articles in that magazine didn't do a thing for me. But those ads, those glorious ads . . . I wondered what next month would bring. A way to shrink my size-ten feet down to a dainty six-and-a-half? Or perhaps a system in a jar to realign my sway back? Age spot removal for hands . . . face . . . entire body?

Ah yes, promises, promises. My whole insides were laughing with glee and optimism as I daydreamed my way right into one big gorgeous hunk of happiness. It was a grand, beautiful hour, while it lasted.

Dancing Lessons

I'd been a single parent of four for five years, and I worried about everything. About whether the sump pump would conk out during a big rain and flood my family room when I wasn't home. About wasps' nests in the overhang and broken tree limbs in the gutter. About how I would put four kids through college, three at the same time. About how I would ever find a nice man to date and how sad it would be to grow old alone.

One Saturday evening the phone rang. It was a man with a deep voice telling me I'd won a free dance lesson.

"It's fun and you'll learn lots of different dance steps," he proclaimed convincingly.

When I hung up the phone, I could feel my face flush. *What if*

I step on my instructor's toes and make a fool of myself?

At class the following week, a woman dressed in a black chiffon skirt and red spangled *Wizard of Oz* high-heeled shoes glided toward me, followed by two handsome young men. She reached for my hand. "Hello, there! I'm Ms. West, one of the instructors. This is Mr. Bates. And here's Mr. Ross. We only use last names here to keep it formal. Ballroom dancing, you know, is very serious."

Serious? I gasped. With giant grins etched onto their faces and their happy feet tip-tapping around the dance floor, they were bouncy, peppy, light-on-their-feet little gremlins. Definitely not serious. This was happy feet land.

"All right," one of the instructors called out cheerily, "everyone join hands and make a big circle. We're going to do the 'push-pull.' Pretend you're squishing grapes. Right foot back, ladies, and squish! Now left foot forward and squish! Pretend you're marching in a parade. Right foot forward, flat on the floor, march! Left foot down, march! So it's squish, squish, march, march."

I did it with the others. Squished my grapes, marched my parade. Squish, squish, march, march. Over and over.

Then we had to do it with a partner. Mr. Bates, one of the most

handsome of the half-my-age instructors, rushed over to take my hand. I felt my heart beating faster while Mr. Bates and I squish-squished and march-marched as I repeated the words over and over to myself with each beat of the music.

But then something awful happened. Mr. Bates started asking me questions . . . while we were push-pulling!

"So how do you like dancing? And what do you do for a living?"

Two questions, and here I was trying desperately to keep my

squish-squish, march-march in order. The minute I opened my mouth to answer, my squishes and marches got crossed. The smile never left his face when I stepped on his toes. "It's okay, Ms. Lorenz. We're going to teach you to do all this automatically so you'll look good on the dance floor. You'll learn the fox trot, waltz, rumba, jitterbug, mambo, cha-cha . . ."

All that in forty minutes? I wondered as I glanced at the large wall clock.

"Are you sure you've never had dance lessons before?" questioned the handsome one. "You're so light on your feet!"

Squish-squish. "No, never did." *March-march.*

"So, what do you do?"

"I," *squish-squish*, "I'm a copywriter for a radio" *march-march* "station." *Squish-squish* ". . . write radio commercials." *March-march.*

"What do you do for fun? Are you married? Do you go dancing very often?"

All this from a man who refuses to tell me his first name? "Well, I don't do" squish-squish "much dancing socially, not married," *march-march*, "haven't danced for years, kinda rusty." *March-squish.* "Whoops . . . sorry about that. By the way, my name's Pat."

Mr. Ballerina didn't flinch.

"You're not going to tell me your first name, are you?" I asked.

Suddenly visions of the movie *Psycho* flashed through my mind. "Well, then, do you mind if I call you Norman?" He didn't answer and the smile never left his face.

When the music ended, the instructors walked each guest, arm-in-arm to the other side of the room. It was time to watch the instructors put on a demonstration.

Poetry in motion. Straight out of the thirties. Arms 'a flying. Legs reaching for the sky. I could just see myself on the dance floor at my cousin's wedding . . . my heel up on my prince's shoulder for that split second while he twirled me so fast my full chiffon skirt would brush my cheek romantically before we ended our dance with his strong hands on my hips as he lifted me high above his head in a stunning spin finish. I was Ginger Rogers and my partner was, ah yes, Mr. Perfect.

Suddenly Norman from the Happy Feet Gang, who looked like he hadn't yet had his fifth high-school reunion, stood before me and reached for my hand as if it were a paper-thin porcelain teacup. He carefully placed my hand upon his forearm as we glided ever so lightly onto the dance floor.

We squished, marched, waltzed, fox-trotted and rumba'd. He kept asking me more personal questions while I tried desperately to keep my unhappy feet responding to his happy ones. I wondered if Norman was writing a book about my life.

After twenty-five minutes of squish-squish, march-march, question-question, talk about me, but not about him . . . Mr. Bates ushered me into "The Room." I knew the minute he closed the door and the four dark papered walls started to squeeze in on me that this was the place where they tried to force you to sign on the dotted line. The dotted line just under the part that said, "Ten one-hour lessons for $650, minus a fifty dollar discount because you're such a swell, happy, light-on-your-feet person."

Norman started talking about my life, my social habits, my children, my lack of exercise, my need for more friends, my cash flow, the trouble I had meeting "nice" men, my career, my lonely Saturday nights and my personal habits.

He talked and smiled. He flattered me. He made taking dancing lessons a synonym for turning my not-so-social life into a blaze of filled dance cards and stand-in-line gentlemen callers.

After reading a certificate on the wall over Norman's desk, I decided to change the focus of his inquisition by asking him why he'd gotten his master's degree in urban economics and was now a full-time dance instructor. As soon as the words were out of my mouth, Mr. Happy got happier. Every sentence he sputtered ended with an exclamation point.

"It's fun! Life is supposed to be fun! Dancing is fun! It's great exercise! It's a wonderful way to meet people! It's . . ." He went on for ten straight minutes and I started to hate urban economics.

At last he took a breath and touched my hand gently as he slid the contract under my fingers. His eyes sparkled. I felt his happy feet tapping under the desk.

I reached for the pen. On four lines of the contract I wrote very slowly in bold, neat letters: *No money. Ain't funny. Too bad. So sad.*

I stood up, smiled a happy smile, grabbed my coat and bounded up the stairs.

A week later I called some friends and invited them to join me for a night on the town. After dinner we visited an old-fashioned sixties rock-and-roll club. We rocked, we rolled, we boogied, we did the Twist. We laughed until our sides ached and danced until our legs gave out. We didn't do one squish-squish, march-march all night. But as I laughed that night on the dance floor, I knew for certain that I was one very happy woman. I did sort of miss Norman, or whatever his name was. But not for long.

Expense Sheet

Mr. Jim Murphy, Editor
First Person Magazine
New York, NY

Dear Jim:

I've enclosed my expense sheet for the last article you assigned to me. Before you suffer anaphylactic shock, permit me to explain the last entry.

Because I'd interviewed Mr. and Mrs.Vanetti so many times on the phone and in person to try to get their story right, I felt the time had come for me to take them out for a little dinner as a token of my appreciation for their time and to put some wax to the few loose strings that still remained in the telling of their story for your magazine. My biggest mistake was in letting Mr. Vanetti choose the restaurant.

He said, "I've heard Berthalotta's is a great place."

I said, "Italian, great. I'll pick up you and Mrs. Vanetti at seven o'clock Saturday night." What I was thinking was: *Italian*. Good. That'll be cheap enough. Entrees are usually seven or eight dollars at Milwaukee's Italian restaurants. I can afford this.

At the restaurant I nearly needed CPR when I saw the menu. The cheapest thing, at $12.95, they were out of. So I decided to order the next cheapest thing at $15.95 for a plate of rubbery pasta shells sprinkled with crumbled sausage and peas, which did not even include a salad.

Mr. V said, "Shall we have a glass of wine?"

I said, "I think I'll drink water."

Mr. V continued. "Better yet, let's order a whole bottle."

I said, "Well, if you really want to." What I was thinking was: Oh, my God, no! Wine bottles are $19 up to $95! Didn't you read the menu? I can't afford this! Please, please, no wine. Whatever you do, don't order a whole bottle!

Mr. V ordered a $29 bottle. *What I was thinking was: These Italians are bonkers! I served a tasty Wisconsin-made cranberry wine on Thanksgiving last year on sale for $3.99 a bottle, for crying out loud!*

Mr. V said, "Shall we get an appetizer?"

I said, "Go ahead, if you want." *What I was thinking was: NO!* NO! NO APPETIZERS! Did you see the prices on appetizers?

Mr. V ordered the peppered pizza-looking thing with goat cheese for $8.95. *What I was thinking was: Goat cheese? GOAT* CHEESE for $8.95? What happened to Wisconsin cheddar for $2.99 for a whole block?

Then it was time to order our entrees. I rattled off the pasta/sausage/pea thing, hoping they'd get the connection between the price of that and the amount of money I was hoping this meal would cost.

Mr. V ordered something with four ugly black clam shells filling up most of the plate with a dollop of pasta in the middle for $17.95, and Mrs. V ordered a pasta dish I could have made at home for thrashers for $1.98, only hers cost $16.95.

Then Mr. V said, "Shall we order salads?"

I said, "It's up to you. But I think I'll have enough with the pasta dish." *What I was thinking was: Salads are $5.50 and $7.50! Can't you read? Do you think*

I stand a snowman's chance in Cuba for getting First Person Magazine to pay for this? If we all three get a salad, that's another $20 for lettuce and a few red peppers. Are you nuts?

The entrees arrived. Mr. V dove in. Mrs. V dove in. I smiled and wished I was home eating chicken noodle soup and a grilled cheese sandwich with my teenage son. But I said, "*Umm.* This is good." *What I was thinking was: I could feed Andrew and me for three weeks on what I'm spending for this one meal! And what about all the starving children in Ethiopia?*

We talked about the story. I took notes. I nibbled at my food and wrote, nibbled and wrote. I decided to eat only half my entree and take the other eight dollars worth of it home to Andrew.

Time to leave. Mr. V said, "Shall we have dessert?"

I said, "Sure, if you want. I'm pretty stuffed myself." *What I was thinking was: Dessert? Are you nuts? I barely make nine thousand a year as a full-time freelance writer and you're thinking about dessert? Get outta here! Please, please, please, no! Don't order dessert! I may have to get a part-time job just to pay for this dinner. No dessert. God, if there is such a thing as mental telepathy, make it work now. NO DESSERT!*

Mr. V said, "I think I'll have the flourless chocolate cake with rum sauce."

I said, "Uh-huh."

Mrs. V said, "I'll just have a cup of espresso."

I said, "I'll pass." *What I was thinking was: Espresso? It's $3.50 for Pete's sake! For a teeny cup of coffee? Where do these Italians get off thinking Milwaukeeans can afford $3.50 for a cup of coffee? Flourless cake? I don't get it! How can it be cake if there's no flour? Oh, my God, it's $6.50! Andrew and I could eat oatmeal with raisins for breakfast for ten weeks with $6.50!*

The espresso came in a cup smaller than my childhood doll dishes. Four tablespoons max. The flourless cake looked like a candy caramel, a soft triangle-shaped dark chocolate caramel sprinkled with powdered sugar.

Mr. V said, "*Mmm.* This is good. *Mmm.* One thing about chocolate, it gives me an instant headache. *Mmm.* But I love it. *Mmm.* Oh, this is good. Oops, here comes the headache. But oh, it's too good to stop eating."

I said, "It sure looks rich." *What I was thinking was: Are you whacked out? It's almost 11:00 PM! How can you possibly eat so much caffeine-laden pure chocolate this late at night, especially when it's costing me $6.50? And how can you sit there eating and drooling without offering us a bite?*

Then the check came: $98.56. I reached for my heart pills. Then I remembered I don't take heart pills. But then I realized I actually might need some before I got home. My heart was beating faster than Mr. V's headache appeared after eating one bite of the chocolate goo. I calculated the tip. What I was thinking was: Fifteen dollars? You gotta be kidding! Fifteen dollars for an obnoxious college kid who spent ten minutes reciting the entire menu while we were trying to read it? My hand shook as I totaled the bill—$113.56? It can't be. It just can't be that much. That's grocery money for three full weeks!

Mr. V said, "Thanks, Pat. This was really nice of you."

Mrs. V said, "Yeah, we really enjoyed this."

I wiped the sweat from my brow and said, "You're welcome. My pleasure." What I was thinking was: *Oh, Lord, I wonder if I can talk First Person Magazine into paying for this dinner.*

Warm regards,

Patricia Lorenz

Sometimes life tosses us situations we can't handle. I've learned that a good laugh helps the bad times disappear or at least welds them into more manageable monkey wrenches. The night after my dinner with the Vanetti's I went home and told my son Andrew the whole story, including what I was thinking each time they ordered something. Andrew started laughing at my tale. I started laughing because he was laughing. That's when I decided to write to my editor, begging that they pay for the dinner. They did. And I learned once again that (A) laughter is the number one way to cure heartburn; and (B) writing a detailed letter that brings out the lighter side of a seamy situation almost always rights a wrong. At least it's worth a try.

Mom's Got a Date Tonight

Ask any separated, divorced or widowed person . . . when you're used to sharing your life with someone, to be suddenly single can be the most devastating, lonely, life-shaking experience in the world. Starting over in a new relationship is the farthest thing from your mind.

In 1987, when my divorce was final after a two-year separation, my children had different ideas. After a couple years of being my dates at movies and fast food restaurants, I heard comments like, "Mom, why don't you join that singles group at church and meet some men?"

I started praying wildly. "Help me, Lord! I don't know how to meet men or go out on dates! Besides, who wants a forty-year-old woman with four kids and a big mortgage?"

But after another winter of being alone in the house every weekend while the teens were out with their friends and Andrew, the youngest, was visiting his father, I worked up my nerve and joined the "Single Again" group at church.

A few weeks later the entire membership went out for a fish fry and dancing afterward. Twenty-one women and one man. And that poor guy danced with every one of us, bless his heart. When the evening was over, he sort of limped out the door, alone.

"Lord, I think fish sticks at home would have been more fun than waiting for my turn with Mr. Trip-the-Light-Fantastic," I whined to the Almighty.

For the next few months I kept my social calendar filled by attending my son's high school basketball games, getting more involved at church and treating myself to an occasional dinner out with other single women friends.

Then one day it happened. A man who advertised on the radio station where I worked invited me out to dinner. I was terrified and my children knew it. Julie beamed, "Mom, he's probably really cute and maybe even rich! (As if *cute* or *rich* mattered.) Maybe he'll take you to a really nice restaurant."

Well, he was rich, all right. Too rich. He not only took me to a very nice restaurant, he mentioned that he owned the place and that it was a tax write-off for one of the state's biggest companies that he also owned. He'd just returned from South America on an art-buying expedition and was anxious to take me to his penthouse to show me his antiques. (Yeah, it sounded fishy to me too.)

Believe me, a woman who had to struggle all afternoon to find one decent *going out to dinner* outfit amidst her suburban wardrobe of jeans and jogging clothes, had no business with a rich tycoon twenty years her senior who celebrated every other topic of conversation with another drink.

"Lord, I'm sorry about the lie. I really do like antiques," I whispered when the date was over.

At home that night, Jeanne, my oldest, was waiting up for me. "So Mom, tell me all about him. Did you have fun?"

I took a deep breath. "Honey, he was just too old, too rich and drank too much to suit my tastes."

"Mother, you're never going to find a man with that attitude," Jeanne quipped.

I prayed a lot that night. "Okay, Lord, I need a little help here. I'm not really looking for a man, am I? Don't I have enough to do with my life without complicating it with another adult? I'm just getting used to the idea of being 'head of household' and I rather like the responsibility. You were proud of me, weren't you Lord, when I learned to use an ax to split wood for the wood burner? And when I revved up the chain saw to cut the wood down to size I felt tall enough to reach up and touch the hand of God. And Lord, after a weekend of wood splitting and sawing I don't have the energy to smile politely, let alone look for a date!"

A year later, after putting over fifteen thousand miles on my little car running the kids all over kingdom come with their myriad activities, it happened again. My second date.

This gentleman owned an advertising agency and we went out under the guise of my doing some work for him. We didn't talk much business during dinner, but when the check came and I offered to help pay, he pointed out that the meal was tax deductible. I didn't feel much like a date after that, but the real clincher as to why I never went out with him again was the fact that the entire conversation centered around his two passions in life: golf and tennis. For a woman who has never picked up a club or a racket, it was a real D & B night. Dull and boring.

When I reported to my kids about that fiasco, Jeanne replied, "Mom, that's what you said about your date last year. You're too picky. Do you like being single?"

"So what's wrong with being single, Lord?" I prayed once again. "Just because I spent most of my adult years being married doesn't mean I can't readjust, does it?"

During the next year my social life got busier, without any more dates, I might add. I ushered for a few musicals at a Milwaukee theater with another single mother, then watched the performances *on the house*. I joined the education committee at church. I did some volunteer writing for a local singles magazine. Andrew and I made new friends when we joined a single parents and children's group that met for dinner and a discussion every week. On Fridays we watched Michael play basketball and Julie cheerlead. On Saturdays we rented movies, popped popcorn and relaxed at home.

The next year another friend called. "You have to meet Ben. He's single, your age, no kids and wants to meet someone who likes quiet evenings at home watching movies on TV. He doesn't go out much but he's very good about fixing things around the house. You might like him."

Like him because he's a handyman? What sort of personality trait is that? I wondered if Mary decided to go out with Joseph because he was handy with wood. "Well, at least maybe this guy can fix my snowblower," I thought to myself.

Ben came over early one Saturday afternoon. We talked for a couple of hours. I could tell right away he wasn't someone I wanted to spend any more time with. Rather than waste his time I explained that I had to run some errands, hoping he'd get the hint and leave immediately. He said, "I'll come with you and then we'll rent a movie to watch later on."

I sputtered a bit, then muttered something like, "Well, if that's what you really want to do."

I prayed again. "Oh, Lord, why am I so wishy-washy? I can't even say No to avoid a long boring evening."

Just as the movie began my children started coming home. Julie

from her babysitting job, Andrew from visiting his dad, and Michael from his job at a local pharmacy.

So there we were in the family room. Me, in my big green overstuffed rocker next to the woodburner. Ben on the couch next to my chair. Andrew next to Ben, Julie next to Andrew. Michael plopped down on the love seat. A few minutes later, Tony and John (Michael's friends) came over and they squeezed in on the couch and the loveseat.

Well now. Wasn't this cozy. Mom, her date, eight-year-old Andrew and four teenagers. Michael kept looking at me sort of funny, like, "Where did you find this one, Mom?" I felt like I was on trial. Ben stood up, rubbed his slicked-back hair and went over to investigate the innards of the woodburner again. He liked that contraption, obviously more than he liked being in a room full of jovial teens, a hip-and-trendy second grader and a woman who yawned a lot.

I wondered what the children thought of him and I secretly wished he'd go home so I could put on my lounging pajamas and get comfortable. I wanted to read the paper and write a letter to my folks. But instead I had to sit there and entertain this humorless gentleman who was probably thinking to himself that he didn't expect a crowd when he asked if he could come over to get acquainted.

I closed my eyes for a second and prayed once again, "Lord, I know my friends and I have been grumbling about my meeting a nice man off and on for years. And now, here's one sitting in my family room and I can hardly wait until he goes home. Why am I so fickle, Lord? Do I really need or want to find someone special and get married again?"

These thoughts kept flitting through my head the entire eight hours and twenty minutes Ben stayed at our house that Saturday. When he finally left at midnight I had to admit that being with someone for the wrong reasons is a lot worse than not being with anyone at all.

When I crawled into bed that night I had a heart-to-heart talk with the Lord. "All right. I know I'm not ready to settle down again. I have four kids to finish raising. I'm already settled. Besides, I like who I am. And the man of my dreams, the one who's easygoing, sensitive, intelligent, interesting, has a great sense of humor and a deep faith, just hasn't come around yet . . . and maybe he never will. And that's okay too. Anyway, Lord, I feel like there's a light burning inside me that's all mine. My light. The one that keeps reminding me who I really am. I think Luke said it best in the New Testament: 'If you are filled with light within, with no dark corners, then your face will be radiant too, as though a floodlight is beamed upon you.' (Luke 11:36 TLB)."

You can just imagine the giant belly laughs my girlfriends and I had when I told them the story about my date with Ben. Somehow the laughter made those long hours with him seem okay. Happiness returned with no regrets.

College Commandments: Economics 101

If you're the parent of college-bound teenagers, take heart. One of two things is going to happen. (1) You are going to get those little buggers, those creatures who think you're the meanest or the dorkiest or the least with-it humanoid on the face of the earth, out of the house at long last. Or (2) They'll live at home, go to a community college and continue to treat you the same way they have since they were twelve, only now they think they should get away with all their bad behaviors because "I'm eighteen, an adult. I can do what I want." Yeah right. Either way, it's time to take a look at this situation, have a good laugh with the other parent if you're lucky enough to have two of you in the same household and take matters into your own hands.

I always knew the day would come when I had to say good-bye to my youngest child and leave him in a dorm room somewhere to begin his college education. It happened in August 1998. I said goodbye to Andrew, not in a home state college two or three hours away as I had to my other children, but in Tempe, Arizona, more than eighteen hundred miles and four days in the car away. It wasn't easy to leave this young man who is tied so tightly to my heart strings, but I took it like a woman . . . who knew that our good-bye in the 107-degree, palm-lined park area outside his ASU dorm was not the end of anything.

It wasn't the end of my parenting job even though I knew he was a legal eighteen-year-old voting, tax-paying man. No, having deposited my other three children off at their respective colleges years earlier, I remembered how it went and within the first weeks of Andrew's college life, I was able to retie my motherhood apron.

Over the years I'd learned that just because they're living away from home doesn't mean they don't need us to keep doing those things that help our birds fly off the branch into adulthood. I'm not talking about sending care packages with cookies, clean underwear and extra dollars stuffed inside a few magazines. No, I'm talking College Commandments. Four things you can't teach your kids while they're still living at home, but within the first few weeks after they leave, it's important to either phone, fax, e-mail or snail mail the following:

College Commandment Number One:

Thou Shalt Not Ever Bring Your Dirty Laundry Home to Mom.

One of the main reasons we send these kids off to college is to learn the three most basic things in life . . . how to take care of your own food, clothing and shelter needs. Since most of them live in a dorm the first year that means food and shelter is taken care of. The very least they can do is start managing their own laundry. Besides, nothing ruins a perfectly good weekend visit with your college son or daughter more quickly than the thought of five loads of their jeans and T-shirts languishing on the floor in the laundry room.

College Commandment Number Two:

Thou Shalt Not Call Your Parents on the Phone Collect.

Or worse yet, a conversation like this: "Hi Mom! Call me right back!" Click. If that ever happens, call them right back and say, "Dear, when YOU have a reason or a need to talk to me, YOU pay for the call and YOU decide how long we'll talk. When I have a reason or a need to talk to you, I'LL pay for the call and I'LL decide how long we'll talk. Now let's start again. I love you." Click.

When my kids were in college (before the era of cell phones) too many parents got sucked in by those 800 numbers and prepaid phone cards that did nothing but encourage long, frequent phone blatherings that ended up costing the folks a fortune and taught the students nothing about fiscal responsibility. These days everyone seems to have a cell phone so long distance costs really aren't relevant anymore. But you can still impress upon them the fact that they don't have to have every single latest cell phoneesque high-tech communications gadget.

Just keep reminding yourself that your college student is a legal adult who is entitled to be responsible for his or her own bills, including their "wants" as well as their "needs." As parents we are not obligated to pay their cell phone bills, give them thousands of minutes a month or encourage *texting*, especially not in class or during the times when they should be studying.

College Commandment Number Three:
Thou Shalt Not Spend Money Frivolously.

Where is it written that campus life includes sports cars, appliances in the dorm rooms, nightly beer and pizza parties, weekly shopping trips to the mall for CDs and over-the-top brand-name clothes and wild, crazy, expensive spring-break vacations? As a parent whose children got through college with grants, scholarships, loans, work-study programs and two-to-three part-time jobs each, in addition to the funds I'd personally saved for them, it seems to me that the education, not the fun, is the most important part of those four years. Until *I* could afford to spend Easter in the Bahamas or Cancun myself, College Commandment Number Three was about as fair as it gets. After they graduate and get a real job, I'll be happy to take a ride in their first car and I'll even throw them a bon voyage party when they want to head south for a break.

College Commandment Number Four:

Thou Shalt Have Thine Own Checking Account to Pay Thine Own Bills.

Checking account, good. Credit card, bad. The checking account teaches them the value of having money in the coffer to pay for the item before they buy it. It also avoids the phone call, letter or e-mail that says, "Mom, remember those shorts I bought just before I left? They're great, so could you buy me two more pairs and send them?" You can do the actual buying and mailing because we parents are warm, loving, generous-with-our-time human beings, but just don't forget to include a note that says, "Be sure to send me a check for $27.50 to pay for the shorts."

There were many days when I missed Andrew desperately after he left for college, but there was one consolation. College kids still need lots more lessons from parents if we're really going to do our job well. I call it College Commandments: Economics 101. Others call it "tough love." My daughter Julia said it best in a letter written to me after she graduated from college. At the top she'd typed, "A parent is not a person to lean on, but a person to make leaning unnecessary." Amen.

See how easy it is to put a little humor into what could be a really rough time? Attack these monumental changes in your life and your childrens' lives with guts, gusto and, above all, laughter.

Don't be afraid to set down some rules even after they've left for college. Now that I think back on those seventeen years in a row that I had kids in college, I laugh until I cry. Especially when I think about filling out all those financial aid forms year after year. Lots to laugh about there, that's for sure. Especially if any of those college financial aid counselors ever took the time to check my math. I wonder if they knew they were dealing with a woman who has never balanced her checkbook.

The Mickey Capers

Over the past forty-plus years since I've been a full-fledged adult, I've learned many lessons, some of them the hard way. One thing I learned the easy way is that one of the best ways to put laughter in your life is to choose friends who are funny.

My dear friend Betsy's mother Mickey, an octogenarian, is obviously the person mostly responsible for Betsy's outrageous sense of humor . . . one of the main reasons Betsy and I have been close friends since 1981. I'm not sure if my fondness for Mickey is because she has a devilish twinkle in her eye every time she comes to visit Betsy from out east or because my own mother died years earlier at fifty-seven and I still think of Mickey as a sort of mother figure. Whatever it is, for some reason as our friendship grew, I decided to start a *gotcha gift* exchange with my favorite surrogate mother many years ago.

Over the years Mickey and I have gift-wrapped the dumbest stuff you could imagine, oddball items found mostly at yard sales and pawned off on each other amidst merriment and mayhem, mostly during the Christmas holidays or birthdays.

One Christmas I stopped over to Betsy's house to see Mickey during her annual holiday visit and to deposit her annual *gotcha gift* under Betsy's tree. If I remember correctly it was a horrible T-shirt I'd fashioned from some red and black knitted afghan squares I'd found at a rummage sale. And, as always, there was a gift for me from Mickey under the tree.

I couldn't wait to see what that year's worthless, goofy gift would be. When the time came for me to open mine, I was shocked to discover not a gag gift but instead a box of Whitman's chocolates, the big box, two layers tall.

"Mickey!" I shouted, "You're not supposed to get me a real gift, you know that. What did you do this for? I got you something stupid, as always. Honestly, you shouldn't have. But you know how much I love chocolate. So this is very, very sweet of you." I couldn't stop gushing over the first real gift she'd ever given me.

I got up to give her a hug, trying to decide if I should open the box right then and there and share it with everyone in the room or if I should take it home unopened and savor each delightful piece of my chocolate treasure. Secretly, I was wanting to take it home and pig out by myself. But Betsy, also a chocolate lover, had other ideas.

"Oh, go ahead and open it now," Betsy pleaded. I knew she wanted to dig in with me so I gave in to save face. As I carefully slid my fingernail under the cellophane wrapper covering the box of chocolates I was secretly hoping that everyone, including Betsy's husband Bob and their two children, Cheryl and John, would take just one piece and leave the rest for me. Carefully, I lifted the lid.

I blinked, then I blinked again. I stared at the box before me. Mickey had done it again. She got me good. That character had taken a bite out of every single piece of chocolate in that big box.

"Well," she grinned. "I just wanted to make it easier for you to know what was inside each piece."

I'm still trying to figure out how she did it without messing up the cellophane. I'm also trying to figure out how to get her back for that one.

The many laughs we've had over that little incident remind me each time that happiness is often wrapped up in a beautifully decorated package called laughter.

And if you're really lucky you'll have people in your life like Betsy and Mickey who are constantly on the lookout for a big whoopa-looza joke to play on you. It's amazing how much mileage and how many laughs you can get out of one silly little practical joke.

Learning to Love Golf

I don't golf. I never learned to golf. I don't even like the basic premise of golf (hitting a small ball with a skinny stick toward a hole you cannot see) and I don't ever intend to take up golf. For me golf is an expensive, boring, overly regimented way to take a walk.

In spite of my negativity toward this sport, I must admit that for many years, basically since 1985 when I became a single parent, I have been asking my friends to help me find a man who golfs. That's because after these many years of being single I want my next husband to be someone who's gone a lot, since when you've had almost twenty-five years of being head of your household with lots of time to develop your own interests, time alone is an important part of your life.

Think about a man who golfs. At approximately four hours per eighteen holes, plus a couple of hours for celebrating at the nineteenth hole and then maybe dinner with his friends afterward, I figure a game of golf is worth almost a whole day to myself. Now if I could just find a pilot who golfs, I'd be in married heaven.

Even though I possess no golf genes, never let it be said that I have a small mind when it comes to this particular sport. I encourage my loved ones to enjoy the sport with all the gusto I can gather. When my oldest son turned thirty, I took him to Florida for our first ever all-alone vacation. I whisked him away from his wonderfully understanding wife and three beautiful children and the two of us spent five delightful days together exploring, biking, hiking along the seashore, pigging out on seafood and, you guessed it, golfing.

Golf is one of Michael's passions in life. And even though golf is the last thing I ever want to do, I have been supportive of my son's habit. Twice I even asked a friend of mine who makes golf clubs for a hobby to hand-craft a couple of skinny sticks for my son. I've given Michael golf balls for gifts, golf shirts for gifts and yes, I actually took him golfing when he came to Florida for that mother-son vacation.

Since it seemed to me that golfing with a partner would be more fun for Michael than going it alone with a whacked-out mother who only wanted to drive the cart, I asked my dear friend Shirley, age sixty-eight at the time, to golf with Michael. It was a match made in heaven. Shirley proved to be on a level of golf expertise very similar to my son's.

It wasn't easy talking that man behind the counter at the clubhouse into letting me go along without paying. "Mister, I am *not* golfing. I've never golfed and I never intend to golf. I don't even like golf. I just want to drive the cart. I will pay for the cart. I just don't want to pay for the golf. I promise I won't even touch one of those skinny sticks. I'm just the scorekeeper." The man wiped his brow and agreed reluctantly to let me on the course.

Gleefully I found my cart, learned how to drive the thing in ten seconds flat and placed my purse, water bottle, sun visor and book in the various nooks and crannies I found on the dashboard.

I brought a book along, figuring I'd have plenty of time to read while Michael and Shirley were doing their thing. Ha! What a joke. First of all, I loved that cart. Forward, reverse, right, left, spin around. I revved that little machine into world-cup competition and had more fun sashaying around that course than I did in the bumper cars at Disneyworld.

"Mom! Don't get so close to the green!"

"Slow down! I'm getting whiplash," Shirley hollered as I cackled demonically, pressing my foot to the floorboard.

After spinning my newfound pleasure cruiser up and down, back and forth and all around every body of water I saw while the two real golfers dinked around the sand traps, ponds, woods and the rough edges of the course, I soon discovered that I had another duty.

"Mom, come on, you have to be the flag holder on the green."

Yes! More fun. More exercise. I leaped from my motorized thronc, ran up onto the green, grabbed the flag, held the flag, waved the flag, marched around a little bit, started singing "I'm a Yankee Doodle Dandy" and tried to entertain myself while those two Arnold Palmer wannabe's tried to get the little ball into the "Ah, now I can see it!" little hole. After listening to a few mild cuss words when the little ball missed the little hole by inches time after time, I'd then replace the flag, race back down to the cart so I could whisk them and their clubs to the next tee box.

No sooner were my passengers hanging on to the cart, when I'd press the pedal to the metal. "Whee! Golfing is fun!" I'd shout to the birds in the trees. Shirley would hiss, "Sheesh, could you slow down a bit?" Then I'd notice that we'd left Michael behind. I'd spin that little machine around on a dime in a flourishing Mario Andretti move to retrieve my son only to hear, "No, go on. Mom, it's okay, I want to walk."

Terrific. Now I have an excuse to do another 180 degree turn. Wonder if I can whip it through here fast enough to miss that tree.

"Holy bat wings, woman, will you slow down?"

"Oh, sorry, Shirley. Can't help myself. I love this little cart! Hey look, there's somebody's ball over there in the woods." I jumped out, ran into the trees, grabbed the ball and tossed it into the back of the cart. I thought to myself, *This is more fun than looking for Easter eggs.*

"I think that was Michael's ball . . . the one he's playing on this hole."

"Oh, sorry." I tossed the ball back into the trees, hoping Michael didn't notice.

"Wow! Shirley, look! Grapefruit trees! Right here on the course. Big ripe grapefruit. I'm going to pick some. Hey, what a perk. You sure don't get free grapefruit when you golf up north."

I lifted my foot off the cart's power pedal with a jerk, giving Shirley's head a balancing forward jolt and ran off to grapefruit tree paradise.

"Sure wish I had a few plastic grocery bags," I said as I scurried up the limbs of one tree whose fruit was just out of reach. I grabbed as many large yellow grapefruit as I could carry in my T-shirt and waddled back to the cart.

"Michael, look! Free grapefruit. Can you believe this? I got thirteen of 'em! I'm telling you, I *love* golfing!"

At the next hole when my son and my friend were discussing some goofy distance calculation and which club to use, I zeroed in on the fact that there were beautiful creatures, besides the skinnystick-wielding Shirley and Michael, prancing around that golf course. I'd seen large graceful herons and egrets at nearly every body of water on the course. And on the last hole the strangest walking, squawking chicken-like bird creatures I've ever seen kept getting in the way of the golfers trying to tee off. Even the *Beware of Alligators* signs posted at each pond, lake and stream on the course made for interesting viewing. Golfing was turning out to be as much fun as going to the zoo.

All in all, it was a day to remember. Michael and Shirley remember their scores. I think they were pretty high. Good job, eh?

I remember how much fun I had. It was like being at Disneyland, a go-cart track, a flag-waving parade, a citrus orchard and the zoo all wrapped into one grand eighteen-hole adventure. Now when people talk about golf, I don't make a face and say, "What, you're going to waste your time and money playing pasture pool, aiming for a hole you can't even see?"

Nope, now when I hear someone mention golf, my eyebrows pop up and I offer to be their driver. Golf . . . what a wonderful sport!

Sure enough, the giggles, guffaws and belly laughs make me one happy momma everytime I go golfing with Michael. But, you know, come to think of it, that was the last time he asked me to go. Oh well.

The Art of Puttering

Laughter, the kind that makes you truly happy, doesn't always have to be the loud, sidesplitting kind. Sometimes our very lifestyles can cause us to giggle inside nearly all day long. When I'm in what I like to refer to as my puttering mood, I'm like a bundle of giggle bubbles just squishing around my insides. I flit from one project to the next, absolutely loving my routineless lifestyle. Puttering keeps me in a good mood. Makes me feel like I get to do whatever I want whenever I want. It's simply delicious to putter. Sometimes when I pass by a mirror on one of these puttering days I'm surprised to see the big grin on my face. Then I remember. I'm happy! Really, truly happy.

Sometimes as I putter around the house doing a lot of nothing,

I actually try to do something productive, like exercise. The older I get, the harder it is to motivate myself to exercise daily. Most weekdays I'm up and out the door by 8:50 AM to walk across the street to the big pool for forty-five minutes of water aerobics. On weekends, however, I'll wake up, open the front door, take a deep breath, thank God for the beautiful sunny day and promise myself that I'll go for a long bike ride after breakfast.

Then I begin what inevitably takes up most of my time. I putter. I love puttering. I can putter longer than any person I know. First I'll make a cup of tea. Then I'll watch the news on TV. Then I'll go to my office and turn *puttering in my office* into a whole new industry. Settled at my computer, I'll answer e-mails, work on a new speech or write a chapter for another book, reorganize my bookcase, file a few papers, check my e-mails again, organize the annual craft fair at the clubhouse across the street, have a snack, change a few sentences in the devotion I'm working on, check my e-mails again, then sort the clothes for a trip downstairs to the laundry room.

"I gotta go for that bike ride," I tell myself. But it's time for lunch. So then I begin puttering in the kitchen. I see the sympathy card on the dining room table for an older man in my building whose wife just died, so I sit down and pen what I hope are heartfelt words.

"Gotta get that bike ride in," I say again, this time out loud. I often talk to myself out loud. Who doesn't? When you live alone you can do anything you want and you can talk out loud as much as you want. Then I remember, I haven't had lunch.

Back in the kitchen I see the empty cardboard box on the kitchen counter. Oh yes, I have to mail birthday gifts to two of my granddaughters. So I putter around the gift wrapping closet, wrap the gifts and then get them ready to take to the post office.

Next, I head down to the community laundry room to throw two loads of clothes into the washers. I pass by the front door and notice the glass on the outside door is a mess of grimy fingerprints. My puttering continues as I reach for the glass cleaner and paper towels.

"Maybe after lunch I'll take a bike ride," I console my nagging conscience.

After lunch I sit down to dash off a note to my three redheaded grandkids in Cincinnati, Ohio. By now the macaroni and cheese lunch is making me sleepy. Time for a thirty-minute nap in the recliner. When I wake up I tell myself that I can always take that bike ride later in the afternoon.

Back in my office, I play my umpteenth online card game of FreeCell, just to get my fingers warmed up for my serious work, I tell myself. I dash off a couple of letters to conference organizers, hoping they'll hire me to speak. Then, for perhaps a solid hour or two I'll work. Write. Think. Write some more.

I look at the pencils in the holder on my desk and decide they all need to be sharpened. "The bike ride! The bike ride!" my conscience nags. It feels as if Jiminy Cricket is living on top of my shoulder, nagging, nagging, nagging.

Time for a cup of tea. A nice cup of Darjeeling (half black, half green) is a good afternoon pick-me-up while reading the mail.

As I pass through the dining room I notice a house plant looks a little wilty so I fill a pitcher and water all three plants. Then I remember there's a dryer full of dry clothes that need folding.

Passing back through the kitchen I glance at the calendar and see that it's time to pay my estimated income taxes. I sit down and write the check. I decide to pay a few other bills while I'm at it.

By now it's 4:00 PM and the sun is low in the sky. "It'll be hard to ride my bike looking into the sun," I argue to no one but myself. "Should I go or wait until tomorrow," I ask myself.

"Just DO it," Jiminy chirps.

"Oh for heaven's sake," I say to the imaginary cricket on my shoulder. "I'll go, but only for a mile. Ten minutes at the most. I need to get back to my office to get some real work done."

I adjust the seat on my spiffy bicycle that I purchased for myself on my fifty-seventh birthday a few years earlier, climb aboard its magnificent lightweight aluminum frame with shock absorbers and take off. Forty minutes later, with eight miles added to my odometer, I return home, sweaty and feeling better than I have all day.

Over the years as I've pursued my lifestyle of daily puttering, I've discovered that it's a fun, often funny lifestyle. Sometimes, for no particular reason, I'll put on a funny hat, stick in my Billy Bob teeth, put on my big black nerd glasses with the white adhesive tape on the nose piece and take my own picture. It's easy. Just hold the camera at arm's length and smile. It's a silly thing to do, I know, but it makes me laugh. Then when I get a dozen reprints of the photo made, I turn each one in to a note card and mail them, in clear plastic envelopes, to my friends and relatives. I know it makes them laugh to see me in such a get-up. And I figure the postal workers who see those goofy photos of me in the clear plastic envelopes must get a good laugh at my expense too. I could single-handedly be helping cure them of a virus, knowing that laughter helps build up your immune system. When I send out my silly self-photos it makes me laugh, but then I guess it doesn't take much to tickle the gizzard of someone who is relatively stress-free and truly happy.

Three things I know for sure. One, I am happy, really and truly happy. Two, laughter is without a doubt an essential component for a stress-free life. Three, if you have all five of the ingredients for happiness, (see the last pages of Chapter Five for a handy recap), you will be happy too. Life is far too short to spend it any other way.

JAICO PUBLISHING HOUSE

Elevate Your Life. Transform Your World.

Established in 1946, Jaico Publishing House is the publisher of stellar authors such as Sri Sri Paramahansa Yogananda, Osho, Robin Sharma, Deepak Chopra, Stephen Hawking, Eknath Easwaran, Sarvapalli Radhakrishnan, Nirad Chaudhuri, Khushwant Singh, Mulk Raj Anand, John Maxwell, Ken Blanchard and Brian Tracy. Our list which has crossed a landmark 2000 titles, is amongst the most diverse in the country, with books in religion, spirituality, mind/body/spirit, self-help, business, cookery, humour, career, games, biographies, fiction, and science.

Jaico has expanded its horizons to become a leading publisher of educational and professional books in management and engineering. Our college-level textbooks and reference titles are used by students countrywide. The success of our academic and professional titles is largely due to the efforts of our Educational and Corporate Sales Divisions.

The late Mr. Jaman Shah established Jaico as a book distribution company. Sensing that independence was around the corner, he aptly named his company Jaico ("Jai" means victory in Hindi). In order to tap the significant demand for affordable books in a developing nation, Mr. Shah initiated Jaico's own publications. Jaico was India's first publisher of paperback books in the English language.

In addition to being a publisher and distributor of its own titles, Jaico is a major distributor of books of leading international publishers such as McGraw Hill, Pearson, Cengage Learning, John Wiley and Elsevier Science. With its headquarters in Mumbai, Jaico has other sales offices in Ahmedabad, Bangalore, Bhopal, Bhubaneswar, Chennai, Delhi, Hyderabad, Kolkata and Lucknow. Our sales team of over 40 executives, direct mail order division, and website ensure that our books effectively reach all urban and rural parts of the country.

SINCE 1946

!

Used to say you agree completely with something

n my back and I'll scratch yours

This idiom means that if you do something for me,

he favour.

st

f someone tells you that you are toast, you are in a

le.

rocks in your head

Someone who has acted with a lack of intelligence

their head.

le your bed– you'll have to lie in it

This means that someone will have to live with the

es of their own actions.

od

Young people with new ideas and fresh approaches

lood.

k

A Young Turk is a young person who is

and difficult to control in a company, team or

on.

button is bigger than your stomach

f your belly button is bigger than your stomach,

more responsibilities than you can handle.

f something is your call, it is up to you to mak.

the matter.

clap with one hand

t takes two.

is mud

f someone's name is mud, then they have a bad

- **Work like a dog**

  Meaning: If you work like a dog, you work very hard.

- **Work the system**

  Meaning: If people work the system, they exploit the state or similar setup to their advantage.

- **World at your feet**

  Meaning: If everything is going well and the future looks full of opportunity, you have the world at your feet.

- **World is your oyster**

  Meaning: When the world is your oyster, you are getting everything you want from life.

- **Worm information**

  Meaning: If you worm information out of somebody, you persuade them to tell you something they wanted to keep from you.

- **Worm's eye view**

  Meaning: A worm's eye view of something is the view from below, either physically or socially.

- **Worth a shot**

  Meaning: If something is worth a shot, it is worth trying as there is some chance of success.

- **Worth your salt**

  Meaning: Someone who is worth their salt deserves respect.

X

- **X factor**

  Meaning: The dangers for people in the military that civilians do not face, for which they receive payment, are known as the X factor.

- **X marks the spot**

  Meaning: This is used to say where something is located or hidden.

- **X-rated**

  Meaning: If something is x-rated, it is not suitable for children.

Y

- **Yank my chain**

  Meaning: If someone says this to another person it means for the other person to leave the person who said it alone and to stop bothering them.

- **Yellow press**

  Meaning: The yellow press is a term for the popular and sensationalist newspapers.

- **Yellow streak**

  Meaning: If someone has a yellow streak, they are cowardly about something.

- **Yellow-bellied**

  Meaning: A yellow-bellied person is a coward.

- **Yen**

  Meaning: If you have a yen to do something, you have a desire to do it.

- **Yes-man**

  Meaning: Someone who always agrees with people in authority is a yes-man.

- **Yesterday's man or Yesterday's woman**

  Meaning: Someone, especially a politician or celebrity, whose career is over or on the decline is yesterday's man or woman.

- **You are what you eat**

  Meaning: This is used to emphasise the importance of a good diet as a key to good health.

- **You can catch more flies with honey than with vinegar**

  Meaning: This means that it is easier to persuade people if you use polite arguments and flattery than if you are confrontational.

- **You can choose your friends, but you can't choose your family**

  Meaning: Some things you can choose, but others you cannot, so you have to try to make the best of what you have where you have no choice.

- **You can lead a horse to water,**

  Meaning: This idiom means someone, like good advice, bu it.

- **You can say that again**

  Meaning: If you want to agree has said, you can say 'You can say so.

- **You can't have cake and the to**

  Meaning: This idiom means that way you want it, especially if you

- **You can't have your cake and ea**

  Meaning: This idiom means that ways. For example, you can't hav standard of state care.

- **You can't make a silk purse out o**

  Meaning: If something isn't very g do much to improve it.

- **You can't make an omelette with**

  Meaning: This idiom means that in or make progress, there are often l

- **You can't unring a bell**

  Meaning: This means that once som have to live with the consequences a

- **You could have knocked me down**

  Meaning: This idiom is used to mea shocked or surprised.

- **You do not get a dog and bark you**

  Meaning: If there is someone in a lo should do a task, then you shouldn't d

- **You get what you pay for**

  Meaning: Something that is very low very good quality.

- **You said**

  Meaning just said.

- **You scra**

  Meaning I'll retur

- **You're t**

  Meanin lot of tr

- **You've**

  Meanin has roc

- **You've**

  Meani conseq

- **Young**

  Mean are yo

- **Youn**

  Mea rebel orga

- **Your**

  Mea you

- **You**

  Me deci

- **You**

  Me

- **You**

  M rep

- **Your sins will find you out**

  Meaning: This idiom means that things you do wrong will become known.

Z

Zero hour

  Meaning: The time when something important is to begin is zero hour.

- **Zero tolerance**

  Meaning: If the police have a zero tolerance policy, they will not overlook any crime, no matter how small or trivial.

- **Zigged before you zagged**

  Meaning: If you did things in the wrong order, you zigged before you zagged.

- **Zip it**

  Meaning: This is used to tell someone to be quiet.

- **Zip your lip**

  Meaning: If someone tells you to zip your lip, they want you to shut up or keep quiet about something.

❖❖❖